MAYAN, INCAN, AND AZTEC CIVILIZATIONS

BY
DR. MICHAEL KRAMME

COPYRIGHT © 1996 Mark Twain Media, Inc.

ISBN 1-58037-051-9

Printing No. CD–1886

Mark Twain Media, Inc., Publishers
Distributed by Carson-Dellosa Publishing Company

TABLE OF CONTENTS

TIME LINE

B.C.

before 8000	Man crosses the Bering Strait into the Americas
8000	Land bridge covered by Bering Sea as ice caps melt
2500	Pre-classical Period of the Mayas
1200	Beginning of the Olmec civilization (Peak of culture 700 to 400)
200	Altiplano Indians begin building city of Teotihuacan
100	Olmec civilization disappears

A.D.

250–900	Mayan Classical Period
600	Olmec and Altiplano city of Teotihuacan reaches its peak
750	Teotihuacan destroyed
900–1200	Toltec civilization
900	Mayas abandon their cities; Post-classical Period
1100	Incan city of Cuzco founded
1150	Toltec city of Tula destroyed
1200	Aztecs begin to settle in the Valley of Mexico
1325	Aztecs found city of Tenochtitlan
1438–1471	Reign of great Incan ruler Pachacutec
1440–1468	Reign of great Aztec ruler Montezuma I
1492	Columbus discovers the Americas
1502	Columbus meets Mayan traders
1519	Montezuma captured
1521–1525	Cortés defeats Aztecs
1533	Incan ruler Atahualpa is defeated by Spanish under Pizarro and is killed
1697	Tayasal, the last Mayan kingdom, falls to the Spanish
1790	Discovery of the Aztec calendar stone
1911	Incan city of Machu Picchu is rediscovered

INTRODUCTION

The purpose of this book is to provide resources for the study of the major Indian civilizations of Central and South America. The mysteries and differences in culture of these civilizations can easily catch the imagination and natural curiosity of today's students.

Each civilization has a general survey chapter. The lesser-known civilizations such as the Olmecs and the Toltecs have only one or two chapters. A series of specialized narrations follow the survey chapter for the major civilizations (Maya, Inca, and Aztec). However, each narrative may stand independently of the survey chapter.

Teachers may choose to use the readings as class projects or as extra enrichment activities for individual students. The activities are designed for students to complete individually. Occasionally, suggestions for group projects have been included.

A short-answer question page appears after each narrative. These questions provide a quick check of reading comprehension. An additional activity follows for each narrative. These activities include word searches, word scrambles, map exercises, crossword puzzles, and others. These exercises serve as tools to reinforce the learning of information in the narratives as well as to develop a variety of skills.

THE ARRIVAL OF MAN

Giant ice caps covered both the Arctic and Antarctic regions of the earth over 50,000 years ago. The levels of the oceans lowered because much of the earth's water was trapped in the polar ice caps. The lower water level exposed a piece of land that connected Siberia to Alaska. Today this area is once again under water and is called the Bering Strait.

Many scientists believe that early men crossed over this land bridge and began to spread out and settle in what is now North America. These people then moved into Central and South America. The Bering Strait land bridge disappeared under the water when the ice caps thawed. This happened at the end of the Ice Age around 8,000 B.C. Today, we refer to the people who first settled in the Western Hemisphere as prehistoric Indians.

As tribes migrated throughout North, Central, and South America, they discovered agriculture and learned how to make stone tools and clay pottery.

The early Indians were hunters and gatherers. All of their food came from plants, animals, and fish located near where they lived. When the food supplies ran out, the people moved on to another area to find a fresh supply. These people had to move constantly to find enough food.

No one knows who made the discovery of agriculture. This was one of the most important discoveries ever made by humans. Their way of living changed forever when they learned to plant and harvest crops. This allowed them to remain in one area for longer periods of time. Since they no longer had to move to find food, they built permanent villages. Huts made of mud and branches provided housing for these early tribes.

Early Indians also discovered how to form clay and bake it to make pottery, which helped them store grain from the harvests. At first, craftsmen made pottery only to store food. The Indians later decorated their vessels to look attractive as well as to be useful.

Scientists called archeologists must solve many puzzles to find out how the early Indians lived. Ancient garbage dumps can give important information about foods that were eaten. Remains of stone spearheads, arrowheads, and tools can also give clues to solving the puzzles. Stones used to grind grain and bits of broken pottery tell us about early agriculture. Scientists make new discoveries each year. Each new discovery helps us to better understand how the early Indians lived.

Name _____ Date _____

QUESTIONS FOR CONSIDERATION

1. Why did the water level of the oceans fall during the Ice Age?

_____

_____

2. How do many scientists believe the earliest men arrived in the Western Hemisphere?

_____

_____

3. How did early man first get his food?

_____

_____

4. What is agriculture?

_____

_____

5. How did the discovery of agriculture change the way ancient man lived?

_____

_____

6. What did early man use to make the buildings in the first villages?

_____

7. Why did early man first make pottery?

_____

8. What was the main difference between early and later pottery?

_____

_____

9. In what unusual place do archaeologists look to find clues of how ancient man lived?

_____

10. What things do archaeologists find in these locations?

_____

Name _____ Date _____

THE ARRIVAL OF MAN—MAPPING IT OUT

Using a globe or world map to help, write the name of the following locations on the map on this page:

Alaska
Arctic Region
Andes Mountains
Antarctic Region
Atlantic Ocean
Bering Strait
Caribbean
Central America
Gulf of Mexico
Mexico
North America
Pacific Ocean
South America

THE OLMECS

The first major Indian tribe of Central America was the Olmec. The earliest Olmecs lived on the Caribbean coast and eventually spread into the central region of the Valley of Mexico. Later they settled in what is now southern Mexico. Their civilization continued from about 1200 until about 100 B.C. The Olmec society was at its peak from 700 to 400 B.C. The Olmecs were important because they influenced later Indian civilizations.

The Aztec Indians gave the tribe the name *Olmec*. It means "rubber people." The Aztecs called them this because the Olmecs supplied them with sap from rubber trees.

Giant carved stone heads found in the area of San Lorenzo are ruins of the Olmec civilization.

Archaeologists have discovered the ruins of two major Olmec cities. The remains of San Lorenzo, the oldest known Olmec city, were found in 1945. The most important discoveries in San Lorenzo were giant heads made of carved stone. The heads are nine feet high and weigh about 40 tons.

A larger Olmec city was La Venta. It was located on an island in a hot, swampy area. The main structure in La Venta is a volcano-shaped pyramid over 110 feet tall. La Venta also has two smaller mounds, a courtyard, and other painted structures. Scientists have not excavated much of the site. Modern development has destroyed most of the ancient city of La Venta.

Scientists found many works of art in both cities. The art works include small carved pieces of jade as well as the giant stone heads. They also found perfectly ground mirrors of polished hematite. Hematite is a glass-like substance created by volcanic eruptions.

The jaguar represented the rain god and was a favorite subject of Olmec art. Many Olmec carvings show figures that are half jaguar and half human.

We still do not know much about the Olmecs' daily lives. They used a form of picture writing. They also had a number system and a calendar. How the Olmec civilization came to an end remains a mystery. The stone carvings were deliberately smashed and then buried. There is no evidence of an invasion of enemies. Did the Olmecs destroy their own cities? Why would they do this? We hope that future discoveries can help us answer these questions and others about this mysterious tribe.

Name _____ Date _____

QUESTIONS FOR CONSIDERATION

1. When did the Olmec civilization begin?

_____

2. When was the Olmec civilization at its peak?

_____

3. Who gave the Olmecs their name?

_____

4. What does *Olmec* mean?

_____

_____

5. The two Olmec cities discovered by archaeologists are:

_____

6. What was the major discovery in the first Olmec city?

_____

7. What is the largest structure in the other Olmec city?

_____

8. What is hematite?

_____

_____

9. What did the Olmecs make from hematite?

_____

10. Name at least three things that we know about the Olmecs' daily lives.

_____

_____

_____

Name _____ Date _____

THE OLMECS—WORD SCRAMBLE

Unscramble the following groups of letters to form words that were used in the chapter on the Olmecs. Then give a brief description of each.

1. berCanbia _____

2. brubre _____

3. naS zenLoor _____

4. aL tanVe _____

5. daje _____

6. tameeith _____

7. raaujg _____

8. melcO _____

9. tezAc _____

10. layVel fo ceMoix _____

11. dncaarel _____

12. tleCnar aiceAmr _____

13. lcovnao _____

14. riosrrm _____

15. ismsyouetr _____

TEOTIHUACAN

Teotihuacan is an ancient city located near Mexico City. It began about 200 B.C. and reached its peak around A.D. 600. Indians known as the Altiplano built Teotihuacan. The Olmec Indians influenced the Altiplano, and many people believe the Altiplano tribe descended from the Olmec tribe. Teotihuacan became the capital of the Altiplano tribe. It once had a population of over 100,000 people.

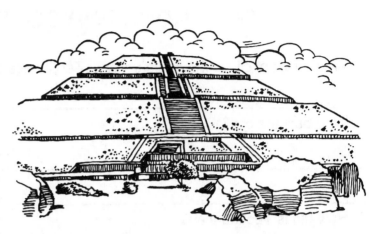

The most famous structure in the Altiplano city of Teotihuacan is the Pyramid of the Sun.

The Altiplano worshipped gods similar to those of the Olmecs. Both tribes used picture writing called glyphs. They also played similar ritual ball games. Both tribes traveled and traded goods over great distances.

The city of Teotihuacan covered over eight square miles. It had pyramids, temples, palaces, markets, and a variety of shops and houses. One unusual thing about the city was its many apartment buildings. Most ancient cities had only single-family houses.

The Altiplano Indians planned Teotihuacan very carefully. Its structures were all built on a grid plan. The main road, named the Avenue of the Dead, connected three of the main temples.

There are four well-known buildings in Teotihuacan. The most famous structure in the city is the Pyramid of the Sun, which is 200 feet tall. It is as large at the base as the great pyramid in Egypt. Another important structure is the smaller Pyramid of the Moon. The Temple of Quetzalcoatl is also an important building in the city. It is named for a serpent god. Carvings of serpents and a god named Tlaloc cover the walls of the temple. The other major building in the city is the Temple of the Jaguars. It is famous for its brightly colored wall murals.

The history of this ancient city remains a mystery. We do not have any written records of the time. The ruins have not provided much information about the beliefs or daily lives of the people.

We do know that they made a special thin orange pottery. Examples of this pottery have been found throughout Mexico, so we know that the Altiplano traveled and traded over great distances.

Mystery shrouds the last days of Teotihuacan. About A.D. 750, the entire city was destroyed and burned. The ancient temples and carvings were smashed. Some historians believe outside tribes invaded and destroyed the city. Other historians assume the priests and rulers destroyed their own city. We may never know the answer.

Teotihuacan means "the place where men become gods." Centuries after the destruction of the city, the Aztecs believed the gods had built Teotihuacan. The Aztecs worshipped it as a holy site.

Name _____ Date _____

QUESTIONS FOR CONSIDERATION

1. What present city is the ancient city of Teotihuacan near?

_____

2. Who built the city?

_____

_____

3. How big is Teotihuacan?

_____

4. What is the main street of the city called?

_____

5. What is the city's most famous structure called?

_____

6. What was Quetzalcoatl?

_____

_____

7. What was Teotihuacan famous for?

_____

_____

8. How do we know that the people of Teotihuacan traveled a great deal?

_____

_____

9. What happened to the city of Teotihuacan around A.D. 750?

_____

_____

10. Who did the Aztecs believe had built Teotihuacan?

_____

_____

Name _____ Date _____

TEOTIHUACAN—WORD SEARCH

Find and circle the following words in the puzzle. The words may be placed horizontally, vertically, or diagonally. They may be spelled forward or backward.

WORD LIST

AZTECS	MEXICO CITY	PYRAMID	GLYPHS
MURAL	SERPENT	JAGUAR	OLMEC
TEMPLE	TEOTIHUACAN	POTTERY	ALTIPLANO
APARTMENTS	QUETZALCOATL	TLALOC	CARVINGS
RECORDS	MOON	MYSTERY	GRID

```
V  L  A  V  M  J  R  K  C  A  R  V  I  N  G  S  B  N  D  D
I  K  M  E  X  I  C  O  C  I  T  Y  Q  Z  R  Z  R  F  Y  T
S  R  Y  Q  U  E  T  Z  A  L  C  O  A  T  L  W  A  O  R  E
K  K  Y  R  B  B  G  V  Y  F  H  X  S  B  O  L  M  E  C  O
T  S  X  T  E  S  I  R  O  N  A  L  P  I  T  L  A  M  I  T
Q  E  X  I  L  T  E  U  O  U  G  X  V  S  B  X  Z  H  L  I
O  C  M  J  K  T  T  W  X  N  O  Q  M  G  T  A  M  K  U  H
W  I  X  P  S  R  E  O  V  L  Z  A  V  T  J  O  V  M  P  U
S  R  S  Y  L  L  D  L  P  B  W  F  J  R  W  M  U  O  M  A
N  G  M  G  U  E  E  Y  T  O  W  R  D  W  Y  F  N  O  X  C
P  H  C  O  L  A  L  T  I  C  G  B  J  N  U  S  D  N  U  A
N  C  H  D  N  R  G  F  O  E  T  X  E  Y  I  U  S  F  N  N
W  D  I  J  M  A  G  D  X  L  A  R  U  M  D  G  R  Y  X  C
P  R  U  C  Z  U  Y  C  L  W  D  I  M  A  R  Y  P  K  Y  L
X  K  O  X  N  G  G  E  X  H  E  D  Z  N  X  D  V  Y  P  I
G  Q  C  D  T  A  E  O  I  U  T  U  R  T  N  E  P  R  E  S
Y  M  D  B  W  J  C  R  O  D  E  R  E  C  O  R  D  S  G  A
B  F  I  S  F  B  V  C  J  E  B  E  D  P  W  G  L  Z  R  H
F  E  R  S  C  E  T  Z  A  S  T  N  E  M  T  R  A  P  A  C
T  Z  G  M  M  U  U  Y  S  H  P  Y  L  G  Q  S  M  Z  G  Y
```

9

THE MAYAS

The Mayan culture spread thoroughout southern Mexico and Central America. It included the Yucatan Peninsula to the north as well as today's countries of Honduras, Belize, El Salvador, and Guatemala to the south. It stretched from the Gulf of Mexico in the west to the Caribbean Sea in the east. This land included rugged highlands as well as dense swamps.

The Mayan people were short. The average height of the men was just over five feet. The women were about four feet eight inches tall. Mayas had straight black hair, and many painted their bodies black, red, or blue. They also often had tattoos. They valued crossed eyes and tied objects from their infants' foreheads to encourage their eyes to cross. Some Mayas also tied boards to the heads of their children to flatten their foreheads.

The Mayas created sculptures on large stone slabs called stela. These carvings reveal much about the Mayan people.

Historians divide the story of the Mayas into three eras: the pre-classic, the classic, and the post-classic. The pre-classic era lasted from about 2,500 B.C. to A.D. 250. During this time, the Mayas came in contact with and borrowed from Olmec Indians. The early Mayan settlements were fishing villages along the Pacific Ocean and Caribbean Seas; they moved inland when they learned to plant crops.

The Mayan classic era continued from A.D. 250 to A.D. 900. They built many great cities, most of which had majestic pyramid temples. Tikal, the largest Mayan city, may have had a population of 100,000 or more. During the classic era, the Mayas improved methods of agriculture. They also developed advanced mathematics and astronomy as well as a system of writing.

One of the world's greatest mysteries is what happened to the Mayan culture. It was the most important civilization in the new world in A.D. 900. Suddenly, however, the Mayas left their great cities and scattered throughout the countryside. We still do not know why the great Mayan civilization ended.

The post-classic era began with the collapse of the Mayan empire. It lasted until the Spanish Conquest in the 1500s. The Mayas continued to farm and trade in the region after the great cities fell. Christopher Columbus met some Mayan traders in 1502. Mayan descendants still live in the region of their ancestors.

Name _____ Date _____

QUESTIONS FOR CONSIDERATION

1. What geographical features did the Mayan lands include?

_____

2. Give a description of what a Maya might have looked like.

_____

_____

3. Why did Mayas tie objects from their infants' foreheads?

_____

_____

4. Why did some Mayas tie boards to their children's heads?

_____

_____

5. What did early Mayas eat?

_____

6. List the three Mayan eras, including their beginning and ending dates.

_____

_____

7. What did the Mayas develop in the classical era?

_____

8. What was the largest Mayan city in the classical era? How large was its population?

_____

_____

9. What is the great mystery of the Mayas?

_____

10. Who met Mayan traders in 1502?

_____

Name _____ Date _____

THE MAYAS—MAPPING IT OUT

The shaded area of the map shows the ancient Mayan empire, and the Mayan cities of Chichén Itzá, Tikal, and Copán. Use a globe or atlas and write in the names of the modern locations of:

Belize
(this will be British Honduras
 on older maps)
Caribbean Sea
El Salvador
Guatemala

Gulf of Mexico
Honduras
Mexico
Pacific Ocean
Yucatan Peninsula
Nicaragua

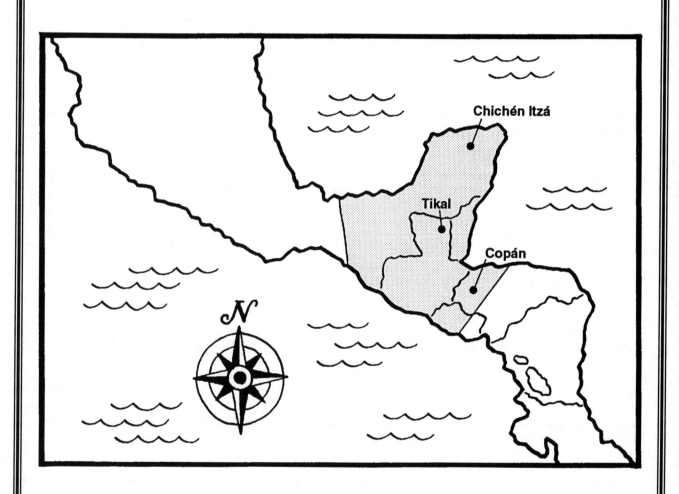

MAYAN RELIGION

Religion was important to every part of Mayan life. The Mayas worshipped many different gods. Each day, month, city, and occupation had its own special god or goddess. The Mayas had a variety of religious festivals and celebrations. Most of these celebrations included human sacrifice.

The Mayan empire was divided into many city-states. Each city-state had its own ruler. His name was *halach uinic*. This meant "the true or real man." The Mayas believed halach uinic was a living god. He ruled until his death. At his death, his oldest son became the next halach uinic. If the halach uinic did not have a son, his brother would rule. If he did not have a brother, the ruler's council elected a member of his family to serve. Some historians believe that the halach uinic also served as the high priest during religious ceremonies.

Each Mayan city-state had a ruler called the halach uinic. He may have also served as the high priest during religious ceremonies.

The halach uinic dressed in elaborate and colorful clothes. He also wore a very large head-dress. Temple wall paintings show him with large ear decorations, crossed eyes, and many tattoos.

Many other priests served with the halach uinic. These priests, named *ahkin*, performed many duties. They had the knowledge of mathematics and astronomy. Some of the ahkin were prophets. Some of them performed the religious sacrifices. Other ahkin performed medical rituals. The Mayas believed that only the priests could explain the mysteries of life and death. The Mayas believed that the earth was flat. They thought it was on the back of a crocodile that floated in a large pond. At another time they believed the earth was the floor of a lizard house.

The Mayas' religion taught that there were 13 layers of heavens above the earth. They also believed nine underworlds were below. They thought that they lived in the fifth creation of the world. The previous four worlds had each been destroyed by a great flood. At the beginning of the fifth world, the gods created humans from corn.

Many of the Mayan religious ceremonies included gifts and sacrifices to the various gods and goddesses. The Mayas believed the gods would give favors to them in return for prayers, offerings, and sacrifices. The sacrifices included valuable gifts, their own blood, and human sacrifices.

In many ceremonies, the priests cut themselves to get blood to present to the gods. The Mayas had three methods of giving the human sacrifices. Often, the priests took the victim to the altar at the temple. Then the priests cut the heart out of the living victim and presented it to the god.

In another method, the priests tied the victim to a wooden pole. Then they threw spears and arrows at the victim's chest in the area of the heart.

In the third type of sacrifice, they threw the victim into a sacred well. The most famous of these wells is the Well of Sacrifice at Chichén Itzá. If victims survived the fall and did not drown, the priests pulled them back out of the well. The Mayas believed the gods had chosen to spare these victims. The priests then asked the victims what messages they brought back from the gods. The victims received special treatment from then on since the Mayas believed they had spoken to the gods.

The Mayas also worshipped the dead. They believed the dead became one with the gods. They worshipped their ancestors at many religious ceremonies. They also built pyramids over the sacred remains of their dead rulers.

THE MAYAN GODS AND GODDESSES

The Mayas worshipped many gods. Here are some of the more important ones:

Itzamná: He was the head god, lord of the heavens and lord of night and day. His name meant lizard. Carved pictures show him as an old crossed-eyed man. He had a lizard's body. The Mayas believed he invented books and writing.

Kinich Ahau: He was the sun god. He was also the god of the rulers.

Chac: He was the rain god. Carvings show him as a reptile with a large nose pointing down and curling fangs. He had four aspects:

Chac Xib Chac	Red Chac of the East
Sac Xib Chac	White Chac of the North
Ek Xib Chac	Black Chac of the West
Kan Xib Chac	Yellow Chac of the South

14

THE MAYAN GODS AND GODDESSES (continued)

Yun Kaax: He is the god of maize (corn). He is also the god of all agriculture. Pictures always show him as a young man. He is either carrying a plant or has a plant as a headdress.

Ah Puch: He is the god of death. Carvings of him show a skull and skeleton.

Ek Chaub: He is the god of trade. Mayan artists painted his face black and he had a drooping lower lip.

Ix Chel: She is the moon and rainbow goddess. She is also the goddess of weaving and childbirth.

Buluc Chabtan: He is the god of war and human sacrifice. Carvings of him show a black line around his eye and down onto his cheek. He is at times shown with a torch or weapon in his hand.

Name _____ Date _____

QUESTIONS FOR CONSIDERATION

1. What did people call the ruler of each city-state?

_____

2. What did the Mayas believe the halach uinic was?

_____

_____

3. What may the halach uinic also have served as?

_____

4. What was the Mayan name for the priests?

_____

5. What did the Mayas believe about the earth?

_____

_____

6. What did the Mayas believe the earth rode on the back of?

_____

7. According to the Mayan religion, what were humans made from?

_____

8. How many underworlds did the Mayas believe there were below the surface of the earth?

_____

9. Briefly describe one method of human sacrifice.

_____

_____

10. What would happen if a sacrificial human were thrown into a well and didn't die?

_____

_____

Name _____ Date _____

MAYAN RELIGION—MATCHING ACTIVITY

Place the letter of the description or definition from Column B that matches the term in Column A on the line next to each item.

COLUMN A	COLUMN B
_____ 1. ahkin	A. the rain god
_____ 2. Ah Puch	B. ruler of a Mayan city-state
_____ 3. Buluc Chabtan	C. the god of trade
_____ 4. Chac	D. Mayan priests
_____ 5. Chichén Itzá	E. the head god of the Mayas
_____ 6. crocodile	F. how each creation of the world was destroyed
_____ 7. Ek Chaub	G. the god of death
_____ 8. great flood	H. where the Well of Sacrifice is located
_____ 9. halach uinic	I. the god of maize
_____ 10. heavens	J. number of underworlds below the earth
_____ 11. Itzamná	K. the sun god
_____ 12. Ix Chel	L. what the Mayas believed the earth floated on
_____ 13. Kinich Ahau	M. the god of war and human sacrifice
_____ 14. nine	N. there were 13 layers of this above the earth
_____ 15. Yum Kaax	O. the rainbow and moon goddess

MAYAN CITIES

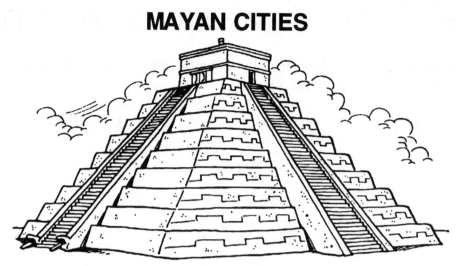

The Pyramid of Kukulcan at Chichén Itzá

The ruins of Mayan cities remained hidden for centuries in the dense jungles. Scientists are still working to uncover and study most of these cities, but visitors can now explore the ruins of Tikal, Copán, Chichén Itzá, and several other cities.

At first, scientists thought these locations were religious centers only. After further study, they found these were complete cities. The ceremonial center formed the heart of each city. Tall pyramids topped with temples stood in large open plazas, and public buildings, palaces, and ball courts surrounded the plazas.

The rulers and priests likely lived in the city's center. The upper- and middle-class citizens built their homes just outside the city center, and the peasants lived in huts on the edges. Raised roads, called causeways, ran through the city. Mayas built the causeways two to four feet above ground level. Some causeways measured up to 15 feet wide.

The Mayas used carved stone for the main buildings of the city. They carved the giant building stones with simple tools that were also made of stone, since they did not have metal tools. They moved the stones to the building location using man power. They did not use animals or wheeled vehicles to help. A cement made of limestone provided mortar between the stones. The Mayas spread a limestone stucco or cement over stones to give the buildings smooth surfaces and then painted the buildings with bright colors.

Tikal, in northern Guatemala, is the largest and perhaps oldest Mayan city. It spread over 50 square miles. Tikal's population may have reached over 100,000 people. The central plaza in Tikal measures 250 by 400 feet. Two of the eight pyramid temples of Tikal face each other across the great plaza. The temple of the Giant Jaguar and its pyramid rise over 150 feet. Scientists discovered a tomb inside one of the pyramids. There they found jade, pearl, and shell jewelry. Inscriptions revealed that it was a tomb containing the skeleton of a ruler named Double Comb.

Copán is the second largest Mayan city. It has five main plazas. The most famous ruin in Copán is the great staircase. It is 30 feet wide and has 63 steps. Picture writing covers each step. Copán also has a perfect example of a ball court.

The ruins of Chichén Itzá include several plazas, pyramid temples, and ball courts. The great pyramid of Chichén Itzá is visible from miles away. An important ruin is the large observatory tower used by ancient astronomers. Chichén Itzá is the location of The Well of Sacrifice. The Mayas threw many live men into the well as sacrifices to the gods.

Name _____ Date _____

QUESTIONS FOR CONSIDERATION

1. What were raised roads called?

_____

2. What were Mayan tools made of?

_____

_____

3. What is the name of the largest and perhaps oldest Mayan city?

_____

4. How big was the population of the largest Mayan city?

_____

5. How many pyramid temples did the largest city have?

_____

6. What is the name of the second largest Mayan city?

_____

7. How many main plazas does Copán have?

_____

8. Describe the most famous ruin in Copán.

_____

_____

9. What city contains the Well of Sacrifice?

_____

10. Name an important ruin of Chichén Itzá.

_____

_____

Name _____ Date _____

MAYAN CITIES—WORD SCRAMBLE

Unscramble the following groups of letters to form words that were used in the chapter on the Mayan cities:

1. kTIai _____

2. noCap _____

3. cehiCnh zIta _____

4. ripmasdy _____

5. pestmel _____

6. zapsal _____

7. neaspast _____

8. wasyausec _____

9. metaGalua _____

10. rugaJa _____

11. lengusj _____

12. onemeilts _____

13. cifeacrsi _____

14. eDluob bCmo _____

15. vtyaeboosrr _____

MAYAN WRITING

The Mayas used the most advanced system of writing of the ancient Americans. They probably borrowed the idea of picture writing from the Olmecs. They then developed their own system of writing based on that.

They did not use an alphabet. Instead, they used a combination of pictures to represent ideas and symbols to represent sounds. The pictures and symbols used in their writing are called glyphs. The Mayas combined glyphs into groups. These groupings have a square or oval shape. We know of about 800 different glyphs.

Scientists study Mayan writing in the few remaining Mayan books and examples carved on stones. Many of these stones are from ancient Mayan buildings. Scientists know the meaning of some of the Mayan symbols.

This is a page from the Madrid Codex, one of the few remaining samples of Mayan writing.

Much of the Mayan writing system still remains a mystery. So far, we know the meaning of fewer than half the glyphs discovered.

Here are some examples of Mayan glyphs:

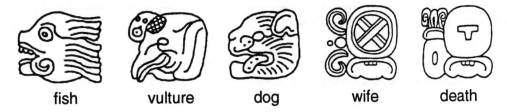

| fish | vulture | dog | wife | death |

The Mayas had a process for making paper that used fibers from the bark of the ficus tree. They pounded the fibers into a pulp then glued the pulp together with tree sap. When the paper dried, they coated it with white lime. This made a smooth, white surface on which to paint.

The Mayas also made books. The name for a Mayan book is *codex.* Mayas used ficus-fiber paper or deer hide for pages. The pages of Mayan books folded from side to side and unfolded like a screen. They painted colorful glyphs and pictures of gods, animals, and objects on the pages of the codex. The Mayas used decorated boards for covers.

Spanish conquerors found great collections of Mayan books, but according to the beliefs of the Spanish, Mayan books were evil, so the conquerors destroyed most of them. Only three complete Mayan books survive today. They are located in museums in Europe. Only fragments of other Mayan books remain.

Name _____ Date _____

QUESTIONS FOR CONSIDERATION

1. From whom do experts believe Mayas borrowed their writing?

_____

2. What type of writing did Mayas use?

_____

3. What are Mayan pictures called?

_____

4. How did Mayas make paper?

_____

_____

5. How did they make their paper white?

_____

_____

6. What were Mayan books called?

_____

7. What did Mayas use for book covers?

_____

8. Why did the Spanish destroy Mayan books?

_____

9. How many Mayan books are still in existence today?

_____

10. Where are the Mayan books that have survived?

_____

_____

Name _____ Date _____

MAYAN WRITING—WORD SEARCH

Find and circle the following words in the puzzle. The words may be placed horizontally, vertically, or diagonally. They may be spelled forward or backward.

WORD LIST

ALPHABET	DEER HIDE	PICTURES	BOOKS
FICUS	TREE PULP	CARVED	GLYPHS
WHITE LIME	CODEX	PAPER	WRITING
SYMBOLS	ADVANCED	SOUNDS	OLMECS
IDEAS	SQUARE SHAPE	TREE SAP	COLORFUL

```
E  B  Z  J  O  T  S  P  P  K  X  P  O  B  O  W  C  H  I  F
V  J  V  D  P  C  C  A  R  V  E  D  X  J  X  E  F  O  D  K
B  Q  S  U  E  F  I  C  V  J  S  D  C  O  D  E  X  W  E  H
O  L  H  M  C  A  I  T  W  O  E  R  J  F  Y  G  H  H  A  C
O  R  L  E  Z  D  P  L  U  P  E  E  R  T  I  I  E  H  S  E
K  O  P  T  S  C  P  N  J  U  J  O  F  W  T  C  Y  O  D  P
S  A  A  R  L  H  D  Z  J  C  Y  K  P  E  X  G  U  Z  Z  A
V  Z  P  L  G  S  Z  U  A  I  X  S  L  C  J  J  J  S  G  H
E  X  E  I  H  Z  C  Y  U  G  R  I  H  T  T  M  B  F  K  S
V  T  R  T  X  H  L  C  R  N  M  I  D  P  M  O  W  W  P  E
G  N  I  T  I  R  W  W  M  E  T  H  V  P  Y  K  Y  I  I  R
D  E  E  R  H  I  D  E  E  K  R  X  F  K  K  L  Q  T  C  A
T  E  B  A  H  P  L  A  W  A  M  D  S  D  M  Q  G  R  T  U
I  V  I  B  O  T  F  C  S  U  D  M  L  H  M  K  G  E  U  Q
Y  N  S  R  L  W  U  P  H  P  U  V  Y  V  N  V  O  E  R  S
Q  T  X  N  R  S  L  O  B  M  Y  S  A  D  H  N  K  S  E  G
E  C  H  H  N  V  D  W  O  I  F  Q  P  N  T  T  N  A  S  M
O  Z  F  P  Z  X  U  V  R  Z  W  W  V  L  C  I  H  P  V  G
U  Y  U  L  U  F  R  O  L  O  C  F  S  S  B  E  H  I  I  X
I  P  E  V  N  T  N  I  P  L  T  F  D  Q  W  V  D  X  B  V
```

MAYAN MATHEMATICS AND ASTRONOMY

The Mayas developed an important system of mathematics. It was more advanced than the systems used by the ancient Egyptians, Greeks, or Romans.

The Mayas were perhaps the first people to use the idea of a zero. This was an important invention. They used a picture of a shell to equal zero. They also used a dot to equal one. A bar equaled five. The Mayas used a base of 20 the same way we use a base of ten. However, they wrote their numbers from top to bottom instead of from left to right as we do.

The Mayas built observatories in many of their cities to aid in their study of astronomy. This observatory in Chichén Itzá still stands today.

Mayan numbers looked like this:

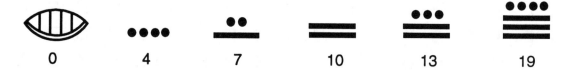

An advanced system of astronomy was also developed by the Mayas. The priests studied the movements of the Sun, Moon, planets, and stars. They could predict eclipses and the orbit of the planet Venus. The Mayas believed that the heavenly bodies were gods. If they studied the sky, the Mayas hoped to learn to predict events on earth that these gods controlled.

To study the heavens, the Mayas built large observatories in many of their cities. The observatory at Chichén Itzá is one of the important Mayan buildings that still stands.

The Mayan priests used their knowledge of astronomy and mathematics to develop accurate calendars. They had two different calendars. One was a sacred calendar, and the other was used for planning regular events.

The sacred calendar had 260 days. It used 20 day names, and each day had a god or goddess associated with it. They did not divide the sacred calendar into months. The Mayas used this calendar to determine religious events.

A 365-day calendar based on the movement of the earth around the Sun was also used. This calendar had 18 months of 20 days each. The Mayas believed the five extra days at the end of the year were unlucky. The Aztecs later based their calendar on that of the Mayas.

Name _____ Date _____

QUESTIONS FOR CONSIDERATION

1. What did a drawing of a shell represent?

_____

2. We use a decimal system using a base of ten. What base did Mayan mathematics use?

_____

3. Write the numbers "eight" and "twelve" the way the Mayas would have written them.

        _____   _____

          eight   twelve

4. What did priests study?

_____

5. Describe the use of the important Mayan building still standing in the city of Chichén Itzá.

_____

_____

6. Describe the two Mayan calendars.

_____

_____

7. How did the two Mayan calendars differ from each other?

_____

_____

8. How were astronomy and mathematics useful to Mayan priests?

_____

_____

9. What did Mayas consider the five extra days at the end of the regular calendar?

_____

10. Who based their calendar on the Mayan calendar?

_____

Name _____ Date _____

MAYAN MATH EXERCISE

The Mayas used a shell to equal 0, a dot to equal one, and a bar to equal 5. Fill in the missing Mayan number symbols.

0	1	2	3	4	5	6

7	8	9	10	11	12	13

14	15	16	17	18	19

Write in the answers to the following math problems, using Mayan numbers:

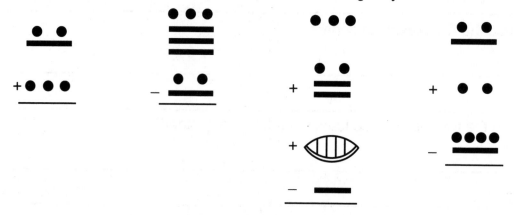

On the back of the page, make up and answer four Mayan math problems.

MAYAN ARTS AND CRAFTS

Nothing remains of ancient Mayan cloth, feather, or basket weaving. Due to the moist climate, all examples of these crafts have rotted away. Remaining pictures on murals, vase paintings, and sculptures show what these crafts looked like.

Only the Mayan women did the spinning and weaving. Cotton was the most common fiber used. At times, the women also wove rabbit fur fibers. They made cloth both for home use as well as something to trade for other objects.

Brightly-colored cloth seems to be something the Mayas enjoyed. They used both minerals and vegetables to obtain dyes. Some colors had special meanings: black represented war, yellow symbolized food, red stood for blood, and blue indicated sacrifice.

Many colorful birds living in the area

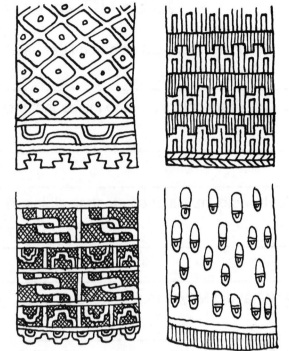

The Mayas developed many brightly-colored patterns to use in their weaving.

supplied a variety of colorful feathers, and with these the Mayas did fancy featherwork. The Mayas used feather weaving to decorate clothing. They also made feather fans and headdresses.

The Mayas wove a variety of baskets from reeds, vines, rushes, and split cane. They also made rush mats and used them for floor coverings. Rope was another important product of the weavers.

Numerous examples of Mayan pottery remain today since it does not decay. Shapes and decorations of pottery changed through the years. Scientists use pottery and broken pieces of pottery to decide the age of the piece.

The Mayas did not use a potter's wheel. Instead, they made pottery from clay coils smoothed together. Cut-out molds were pressed onto the pots to create designs. Mayas made a great variety of pottery. Some pieces were as tall as an adult human.

Mayan sculpture has also lasted through time. Limestone was the most often used material for sculpture. Clay and wood carvings were used for decoration. The Mayas never developed metal work. They used stone tools to carve. The most famous Mayan carvings appear on tall stones called *stela*. Stela still remain in the ruins of the Mayan cities.

Painting was another major Mayan art form. Scientists have discovered brightly colored murals on the walls of Mayan buildings. The murals are frescoes. The artists applied the paint while the walls were still wet. Mayan murals portrayed everyday scenes as well as religious ceremonies.

Name _____ Date _____

QUESTIONS FOR CONSIDERATION

1. What was the most common fiber used for Mayan cloth?

_____

2. List some colors and the things that those colors represented in Mayan weaving.

_____

_____

3. How did Mayas decorate their clothing?

_____

_____

4. What did Mayas make baskets from?

_____

5. How did Mayas make their pottery?

_____

_____

6. How tall were some pieces of Mayan pottery?

_____

7. What was the material used most often for Mayan sculpture?

_____

8. What are the tall stones called that Mayan carving appears on?

_____

9. What types of mural paintings did Mayas do?

_____

10. What did the murals portray?

_____

_____

Name _____ Date _____

MAYAN MURALS

Below are drawings of three of the murals from a temple in the Mayan city of Bonampok. On a large piece of paper, draw and color or paint a copy of one of the murals. You could also create your own mural in the style of Mayan art. Perhaps a bulletin board could be made of Mayan-style murals.

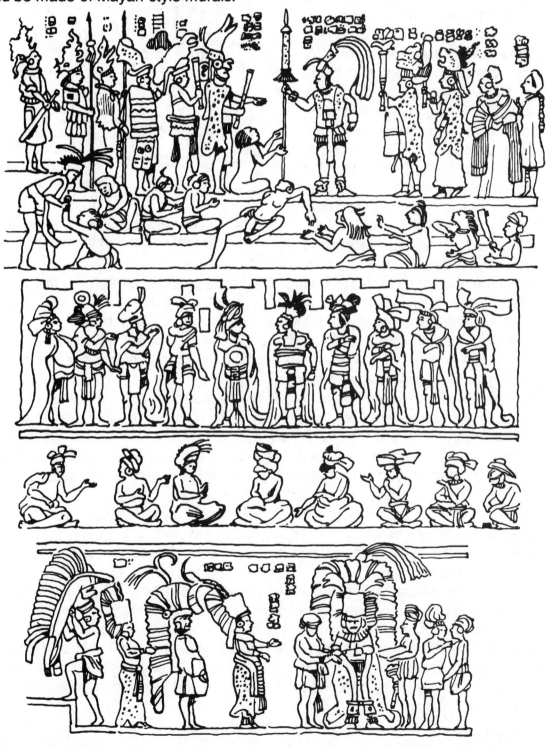

MAYAN AGRICULTURE

The Mayas used a variety of methods to obtain food. Which method they used depended on their location, since, for instance, methods used in the forest regions did not work in the swamps.

The earliest Mayas were hunters and gatherers. They fished and hunted for food. Wild animals they hunted included birds, rabbits, monkeys, and deer. The Mayas also picked or gathered wild fruits, nuts, and vegetables, but hunting and gathering alone could not provide enough food as the population increased. The Mayas then had to plant crops to survive.

A method known as slash and burn is one of the oldest methods of farming. Men cut forests down with stone axes and then let the trees dry thoroughly. The men

Mayan farmers used planting sticks to make holes in the soil for the seeds. Corn was the main crop of the Mayas.

then burned the dried trees to clear the land. The ashes provided fertilizer for the soil. The Mayas planted seeds, mainly maize or corn, using a planting stick. The farmers used the stick to make a hole in the soil and put three or four seeds into each hole.

The slash and burn method wore out the soil quickly. The fields had to be in fallow, or at rest, for two or three years before replanting. In addition to planting field crops, the Mayas also had fruit orchards and vegetable gardens.

Mayas raised a variety of crops. In addition to maize, they grew beans, chilis and other peppers, squashes, tomatoes, avocados, and pumpkins. In some regions at the edges of the empire, they grew cacao plants. The cacao plant was hard to grow, and its beans were valuable since they could be made into a Mayan delicacy called chocolate. In addition to food crops, Mayan farmers also grew hemp to make rope and cotton to make cloth.

Water for the crops was always a concern. Droughts often destroyed the crops. The Mayas built water reservoirs using man-made dams and created irrigation systems, but these were on a smaller scale than those of the Incas or Aztecs. They also built some terraces to help stop erosion.

The Mayas developed a special way of growing crops in the swampy areas. Workers dug soil up into mounds. They then planted and harvested the crops on the mound areas. The ditches they dug out provided canals around the mounds for irrigation.

Religion played an important part in Mayan farming. The priests chose the special days for planting and harvesting. The Mayas had special celebrations and rituals in honor of Chac, the god of rain. They believed that he would send the much-needed rain if the celebrations pleased him.

Name _____ Date _____

QUESTIONS FOR CONSIDERATION

1. How did early Mayas get food?

_____

2. Why did they start farming?

_____

3. What is one of the oldest methods of farming?

_____

4. How was the method in #3 done?

_____

_____

5. In what way was the method in #3 bad?

_____

_____

6. What did the Mayas grow in addition to field crops?

_____

7. Did Mayas grow anything that wasn't edible? If so, name any and tell how they were used.

_____

_____

8. What caused Mayan farmers difficulty?

_____

_____

9. How did Mayas farm swampy regions?

_____

_____

10. Why did Mayas worship Chac?

_____

_____

Name _____ Date _____

MAYAN AGRICULTURE—WORD SCRAMBLE

Unscramble the following groups of letters to form words that were used in the chapter on Mayan agriculture:

1. shertun _____

2. tehragres _____

3. belegsatve _____

4. tlanpign kisct _____

5. dorhascr _____

6. zamie _____

7. vadcoosa _____

8. oacca _____

9. iiirrotnag _____

10. reetcars _____

11. spmwas _____

12. etoolhcca _____

13. srsroeivre _____

14. pehm _____

15. omdsnu _____

MAYAN TRADE

The Mayas became great traders. The Mayan name for merchants was *ppolm.* These ppolm became highly respected and important members of Mayan society. They even had their own god, Ek Chaub.

Trade routes developed throughout the Mayan lands. Later, trade went as far south as Guatemala and Belize. Trade also extended to the Caribbean Islands.

Human caravans carried the trading goods. The Mayas did not use animals or wheeled vehicles to move goods. Instead, slaves did most of the carrying.

The Mayas used large seagoing canoes to carry on trade in the Gulf of Mexico and the Caribbean.

In the interior, small pathways criss-crossed the land. The Mayas did not build major road systems, but they did build canoes for river travel. The rivers provided a faster and more efficient way to move goods.

On the coastal regions, Mayas used large seagoing canoes. Christopher Columbus saw a Mayan canoe in 1502, during his fourth voyage to the Americas. He recorded that it was over 50 feet long and about eight feet wide and had a cabin structure and a crew of about 12 men.

Most of the Mayan trade was directly between merchants, who then resold goods. Some villages became major trading centers. The villagers built large stone warehouses in which goods were stored. Larger Mayan cities had great marketplaces. One of the most famous markets was in the Court of a Thousand Columns. This was a plaza next to the Temple of the Warriors in Chichén Itzá.

The Mayas used the barter system. Barter is the exchange of certain goods for others. Money is not used in this system. The Mayas did not have money. At times, they used cacao beans instead of money. One record shows that a slave was worth 100 cacao beans.

The Mayas traded fruits and vegetables as well as salt, honey, dried fish, turtle eggs, deer meat, and birds. They also exchanged many non-food items. Popular goods included cotton cloth, animal skins, feathers, shells, gold, emeralds, jade, and other valuable stones. The Mayas also bought and sold slaves at the markets.

No other ancient American group became as involved in trade as the Mayas. It was not until modern days that trade again became as important to our culture.

Name _____ Date _____

QUESTIONS FOR CONSIDERATION

1. What did Mayas call merchants?

_____

2. Who was the merchants' god?

_____

3. How far south did Mayan merchants travel?

_____

4. How far east did Mayan merchants travel?

_____

5. How did merchants transport goods over land?

_____

_____

6. Describe a typical Mayan overland road system.

_____

_____

7. Describe a Mayan canoe.

_____

_____

8. Where was the most famous Mayan marketplace, and what was it called?

_____

_____

9. Did Mayas buy or trade their goods? What was their system called?

_____

_____

10. What did Mayas sometimes use in place of money?

_____

_____

Name _____ Date _____

MAYAN TRADE—WORD SEARCH

The Mayas were important traders. This puzzle lists things that the Mayas traded. Find and circle the following words in the puzzle. The words may be placed horizontally, vertically, or diagonally. They may be spelled forward or backward.

WORD LIST

BIRDS	FEATHERS	JADE	CLOTH
FISH	DEER	GOLD	PRECIOUS STONES
SHELLS	EMERALDS	HONEY	TURTLE EGGS
FRUIT	VEGETABLES	SALT	ANIMAL SKINS
SLAVES	CACAO BEANS		

```
B C R H V T M L Y E V P M M W T D C A X
A U U F E S M E S N A E B O A C A C K A
X O S H G T P R E C I O U S S T O N E S
S J T R E D I L W H F Z S C E E V K O R
B D M P T Y U L Y Y S L A V E S S A L T
M C F G A F X B S X F L Q T F O R E E D
M S R H B N I I S L M Q D V I V Y Y V H
H Q U Q L B X R R G U V N M S C S O O Z
O E I J E I G D W G G U Y J H D T N G E
N H T S S E L S R K G E E D A J O X A I
E A G E N S Q H Z P T G E U C I F Y M G
Y G H M B I L S P B Q H U L E N Z M B J
F N K L F T K L J G J R T T A A E D N
Z D C G L C Y S E T U M E J H R T L I D
Y C A P M M F E L H U L D L O G U N G I
F D B T B H B D F A S K K T H K L T E D
X X E M E R A L D S M S M M T M N N P P
G S J R S D X Q S Q L I H H O K F R W H
V X K P X P A V Q G A J N C L Y Z E M X
J F E A T H E R S M H E D A C Z T O M Q
```

THE GREAT MAYAN MYSTERY

One of the great mysteries in the history of civilization is what happened to the Mayas. The Mayas suddenly abandoned their cities about A.D. 850. The Mayan society collapsed, and the people scattered through the countryside. Scholars have formed many theories about the cause of the collapse. However, not one bit of proof of any of these theories exists.

Some people believe that a natural disaster caused the Mayas to desert the cities. Perhaps an earthquake or a hurricane forced them to leave suddenly. Was an epidemic of a disease such as yellow fever the cause? Perhaps they had to leave so quickly that no one had time to carve stones that would tell the story.

Others believe that the Mayas left due to agricultural reasons. Perhaps the

Tikal, in northern Guatemala, was the largest Mayan city. It and the other Mayan cities were abandoned in about A.D. 850.

Mayan system of farming exhausted the soil. The crops could no longer feed the large population. The Mayas did not develop new planting methods. They always used the planting stick. They never discovered how to use a plow. This limited the size of the crops. The Mayas did not use animals nor wheeled vehicles. The only way to transport food from the fields to the cities was by manpower. This limited how far away from the city the Mayas could plant crops. If this theory is true, the people had to leave the cities to avoid hunger.

Another theory is that the peasants may have revolted against the rulers. The peasants worked very hard. Most of their labor provided food and wealth to the upper classes. Did the peasants refuse to continue their work? The upper classes would have had to leave the cities to survive if the peasants left the farms.

Still other people believe that invaders attacked and conquered the cities. Perhaps other tribes such as the Toltecs took over the cities and forced the Mayas to leave.

The mystery of the last days of the Mayas is still being debated. We have no proof of any one of the theories. Will scientists discover something in the Mayan ruins that will give us a clue to the answer? Will we ever find the answer to the great mystery of the Mayas?

Name _____ Date _____

QUESTIONS FOR CONSIDERATION

1. When did the great Mayan civilization end?

_____

2. Where did the people go?

_____

3. What natural causes may have forced the Mayas to leave their cities?

_____

_____

4. Why might agriculture have been the cause of the people leaving the cities?

_____

_____

5. What invention might have increased crop production?

_____

6. How did the Mayas carry food to the cities?

_____

_____

7. What type of revolt may have occurred?

_____

8. Why would a revolt possibly have taken place?

_____

_____

9. What tribe may have attacked the Mayas?

_____

10. Knowing what you do about the Mayas, which theory in the text do you personally feel is the best? Why?

_____

_____

Name _____ Date _____

THE GREAT MAYAN MYSTERY—CROSSWORD

Use the clues below to complete the crossword puzzle.

ACROSS

2. A natural disaster that is caused by the ground shifting

7. The exhausted soil may not have been able to feed the _____ .

9. The Mayan people continued to live in the _____ .

12. This type of fierce storm might have forced the Mayas to leave their homes.

14. A tribe of Indians that may have taken over the Mayan cities

DOWN

1. About A.D. 850, Mayan _____ collapsed.

3. A possible explanation

4. Mayas used this to plant crops.

5. This was the only way the Mayas had to transport food.

6. The name of the great civilization whose finish remains a mystery.

7. A class of people that worked hard to provide wealth and food for others.

8. Mayan farmers did not use the _____ .

10. A _____ disaster may have caused the Mayas to leave their cities.

11. Unfriendly people coming into a territory from outside

13. A major outbreak of disease

THE MAYAS AND THE SPANISH

After the fall of the great Mayan cities, the Mayan people continued to live in both the highlands and lowlands of their ancestors. However, they never again achieved the greatness of the earlier Mayan civilization. Mayapan became the new capital in the 13th century. It was the only walled city built by the Mayas. Mayapan lasted only until about 1441, when it was destroyed.

The Mayas settled in several other small villages. They no longer had a central government. Many independent tribes formed separate city states. The Mayas continued to fight amongst themselves. These civil wars, as well as epidemics, droughts, and hurricanes, continued to weaken the Mayan tribes.

In addition to meeting natives of the Caribbean as shown here, Columbus also reported seeing natives in trading canoes that we now know were from the Mayan civilization.

The first meeting of Mayas and Europeans occurred in 1502. During his fourth voyage, Columbus wrote of seeing native trading canoes. Other white men came through the Mayan lands during the next few years, searching for gold and slaves.

The white men brought with them diseases that were new to the Indians. Smallpox was the worst of these. The Indians had no resistance built up against the deadly disease. The vaccine against smallpox was not developed until centuries later, and hundreds of thousands of Indians soon died of the disease.

The death of so many Indians and fighting between the tribes helped the Spanish conquer the land. Hernando Cortés led several conquest groups through the Mayan lands between 1519 and 1525. Other Spanish expeditions followed. By 1542 the Spanish had built their own capital city, Mérida. Mérida is now the capital of the state of Yucatan, Mexico.

The conquest of the Mayas lasted for many years. It was a bloody and brutal defeat. The Mayas could not compete against the superior arms and cavalry of the enemy. Often, some Mayan tribes joined the Spanish against other tribes. The Mayan armies lost many soldiers to disease.

After a short battle, the Spanish conquered the last Mayan kingdom, Tayasal, in 1697. With the fall of Tayasal, the Spanish destroyed the last remnants of the once great Mayan civilization.

Name _____ Date _____

QUESTIONS FOR CONSIDERATION

1. What was the name of the new Mayan capital?

_____

2. When was the new capital destroyed?

_____

3. What four things continued to weaken the Mayan civilization?

_____

_____

_____

4. What did white men come in search of?

_____

5. What did white men bring with them to the Indians?

_____

6. How many Indians died of smallpox?

_____

7. Who was one leader of the Spanish conquest of the Mayas?

_____

8. What was the Spanish capital city named?

_____

9. When did the Spanish conquer the last Mayan kingdom?

_____

10. What was that kingdom's name?

_____

Name _____ Date _____

THE MAYAS AND THE SPANISH—WORD SCRAMBLE

Unscramble the following groups of letters to form words that were used in the chapter on the Mayas and the Spanish:

1. paaynaM _____

2. medpiesic _____

3. bumClous _____

4. nasceo _____

5. palmxols _____

6. noedarHn restCo _____

7. dearMi _____

8. unqecost _____

9. ralyvac _____

10. lasTyaa _____

11. inhSspa _____

12. vealss _____

13. seedais _____

14. ptneiseioxd _____

15. atYaucn _____

THE TOLTECS

Small tribes of Indians scattered throughout the central Mexico region after the fall of the great city Teotihuacan. Wandering tribes also moved into the Valley of Mexico from the northern regions. One group soon became the most important and powerful tribe in the region. Today we call the people of this tribe Toltecs. Their civilization lasted from about A.D. 900 to 1200.

The first great ruler of the Toltecs was Mixcoatl. His son, Topiltzin, became a legendary figure. He founded the city of Tula. Tula is about 60 miles north of Mexico City. Tula means "place of the reeds." It soon became the capital and largest city of the Toltecs.

Toltec legends say Topiltzin was a peaceful ruler. His god was Quetzalcoatl, a peaceful, feathered snake. His enemies worshipped the war-loving god Tezcatlipoca. Topiltzin and his followers lost to the warlords and had to leave the city.

With the departure of Topiltzin, the Toltecs soon became fierce warriors. They built a society ruled by the military. They demanded tributes from the people whom they conquered. Many of the captives of war became

The Temple of Quetzalcoatl in Tula was adorned with carved stone columns that supported its roof.

sacrifices to the gods, since the Toltecs had begun to include human sacrifices in their religious ceremonies. A sculpture of a skull rack remains in the ruins of Tula. This is a reminder of these ceremonies.

The Toltecs had contact with the Mayas. Trade existed between the cities of Tula and Chichén Itzá in Yucatan. Similar styles of art appear in the ruins of both cities.

The ruins of Tula contain several pyramids and temples. The most famous is the Temple of Quetzalcoatl, the feathered serpent god of Topiltzin and his followers. Large stone columns carved in the forms of serpents and humans supported the roof of the temple.

The Toltec citizens suffered from serious droughts. This weakened their military strength. Outside tribes then conquered the Toltec cities. These enemies destroyed Tula in about 1150. Many years later, the Aztecs reused parts of the buildings of Tula in their cities. The Toltecs greatly influenced the Aztecs. In addition to the Aztecs, many other tribes proudly claimed to descend from the Toltecs.

Name _____ Date _____

QUESTIONS FOR CONSIDERATION

1. How long did the Toltec civilization last?

_____

2. Who was the first great ruler of the Toltecs?

_____

3. Who was the founder of the capital and largest Toltec city?

_____

4. What was the capital of the Toltec empire named?

_____

5. Describe a typical male Toltec.

_____

_____

6. What types of sacrifices did Toltecs offer in their religious ceremonies?

_____

7. What is the most famous ruin of the Toltecs?

_____

8. When was the capital of the Toltec empire destroyed?

_____

9. What people later used parts of the Toltec buildings when they built their cities?

_____

10. Have any tribes claimed to descend from the Toltecs? If so, name them.

_____

_____

Name _____ Date _____

THE CITY OF TULA MAZE

Can you find your way through the maze of the Toltec city of Tula?

START HERE

THE INCAS

The early history of the Incas is a mystery. Since the Incas never developed a system of writing, we must rely on the writings of their Spanish conquerors for any Incan history that we know. We can also study artifacts of the ancient cities for clues to the early Incas' story.

We do know some Incan myths. One early story is that the sun god created the first Incan, Manco Capac, and his sister. The god told them to go and teach other Indians. They went into the wilderness to establish a city. They named their city Cuzco, and it became the capital of the Incan empire.

The Incas probably began as one of many small tribes in the Andes Mountains. At its peak, the Incan empire spread through parts of what are now Peru, Ecuador, Chile, Bolivia, and Argentina. The Incan land included desert, fertile valleys, some rain forests, and the Andes Mountains.

The Incas conquered a vast empire in South America, constructed a 12,000-mile road system, and developed terrace farming and irrigation systems.

The Incas conquered most of their territory under the leadership of Pachacutec, who ruled from 1438 to 1471. The Incas crushed most of the other tribes during brutal fighting.

The Incan empire was so large that they built a system of roads that stretched over 12,000 miles. The Incas did not use wheeled vehicles on their roads. The great road system was for pedestrians. Only the road system of the ancient Romans was equal to that of the Incas.

The Incas developed terrace farming. They cut terraces into the steep sides of the mountains to create more farm land. They also dug irrigation systems to bring water from the mountain streams to the terraces. Many of the Incan roads, terraces, and irrigation ditches are still in use today.

The llama was an important animal for the Incas. They tamed the llama and used it for transportation of men and materials. The llama also provided the Incas with wool and food.

The Incas developed a counting system that used a based of ten. They used a *quipus* to remember numbers. The quipus had a main cord about two feet long. They tied many colored strings to the main cord. Each string had knots tied in it. The color of the strings and the distance between the knots had special meanings.

The Incan civilization was at its peak when the Spanish arrived. Francisco Pizarro led the Spanish invaders against the Incas. After a series of fierce battles, the Spanish defeated the Incan king, Atahualpa, and in 1533 he was killed. The descendants of the Incas, like those of the Mayas and Aztecs, continued to live under the rule of the Spanish.

Name _____ Date _____

QUESTIONS FOR CONSIDERATION

1. Why is so little known about the early history of the Incas?

_____

_____

2. According to legend, who was the first Incan?

_____

3. What was the capital of the Incan empire named?

_____

4. Where is it believed that the Incan tribe began?

_____

5. Under whose reign did the Incan empire grow most?

_____

6. What did the size of the empire compel the Incas to do?

_____

_____

7. How did the Incas grow crops in the mountains?

_____

_____

8. How was the llama beneficial to the Incas?

_____

_____

9. What Incan invention helped with counting?

_____

10. Who defeated the Incas?

_____

Name _____ Date _____

THE INCAS—MAPPING IT OUT

The Incan empire included parts of the countries that are now Peru, Ecuador, Chile, Bolivia, and Argentina.

1. Using a globe, atlas, or map, label those countries on the map on this page.

2. Use a colored pencil or crayon and color in these countries to show the approximate size of the Incan empire.

3. Label the locations of the following: The Caribbean Sea, the Atlantic Ocean, and the Pacific Ocean.

INCAN RELIGION

Like the other Indian tribes, the Incas worshipped many gods and goddesses. The major Incan god was the god of nature, Viracocha, the creator.

Another Incan god was Inti, the sun god. Gold was the symbol of Inti. The sun god temple is the most important structure in Cuzco, the major city of the Incas. The Incas believed Inti was the father of Incan rulers. They worshipped the ruler as a living god.

Major Incan goddesses included those of the earth and the sea. The Incas also worshipped many lesser gods and goddesses. These included gods of thunder, the Moon, stars, rainbows, and others.

The Incas believed they could learn the will of the gods by divining. Divining is studying objects to find magic signs. Priests would look at things such as animal organs,

Winged attendants of the thunder god are shown in profile rather than full face. The figures have rayed headdresses and carry staffs.

flames of a fire, or movements of animals, and from these they would try to discover if it was a good day for planting crops, going to war, or making other important decisions.

In addition to the gods and goddesses, the Incas worshipped *huacas.* A huaca was a scared place or thing. Huacas included mummies of the dead, temples, holy places, and things of nature such as mountains, springs, and stones. Each Incan family had small statues in their homes of huacas. The statues were sacred to that family.

Religious ceremonies were an important part of Incan life. Each family had daily prayers to their huacas. The priests performed daily ceremonies at the various temples. The high priest was a favorite relative of the ruler.

The Incas held a major religious festival during each of the 12 months of their calendar. The Incan year began in December with the Capac Raimi. This means "the magnificent festival." This was the most important and elaborate of all celebrations. Pauca Huaray, in March, celebrated the ripening of the earth. The June ceremony of Inti Raimi was the festival of the Sun. Uma Raimi, the festival of the water, occurred in October.

Some rituals happened inside the temples. The great monthly festivals occurred outdoors. All of the people could take part in them. The celebrations included dancing, feasts, games, songs, and parades. The ceremonies also included sacrifices and offerings. Incas sacrificed animals such as the llama and guinea pigs. At times human sacrifices, including child sacrifices, were part of the rituals.

Name _____ Date _____

QUESTIONS FOR CONSIDERATION

1. Who was the major Incan god?

_____

2. What was the name of the sun god?

_____

3. What was the sun god's symbol?

_____

4. What is divining?

_____

_____

5. What was a huaca?

_____

_____

6. How many months did the Incas have in their calendar?

_____

7. What events were held each month?

_____

8. What was the most important festival? When was it held?

_____

_____

9. Where did the festivals take place? Why?

_____

_____

10. What types of things were sacrificed at festivals?

_____

_____

Name _____ Date _____

INCAN RELIGION—ACTIVITY

Mosaics

Materials needed: large sheet of paper, pieces of colored paper, scissors, and paste.

On this page are illustrations taken from Incan temples. These are of four of the Incan gods. Using a marker or crayon, create a large drawing of one of these gods. It does not have to be an exact copy. If you would prefer, make your own drawing of a figure using the Incan style. Next, cut pieces of various colors of paper and glue them into the spaces created by your drawing. You have made a mosaic. Ancient artists used various colored stones to make their mosaics.

The eye areas of the mosaic could be cut out and string attached to the sides to make a mask to wear. Perhaps you and your classmates could make a bulletin board of the mosaics you make.

GOD OF THUNDER AND LIGHTNING

MOTHER EARTH GODDESS

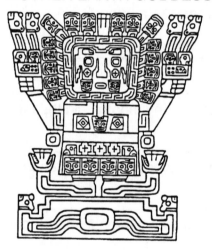

SUN GOD

MOON GODDESS

INCAN AGRICULTURE

Many of the foods we use today were also part of the Incan diet. Incan farmers grew a greater variety of crops than any other ancient American tribe. They grew potatoes, corn, tomatoes, avocados, peppers, strawberries, peanuts, cashews, squash, beans, pineapples, chocolate, and other crops.

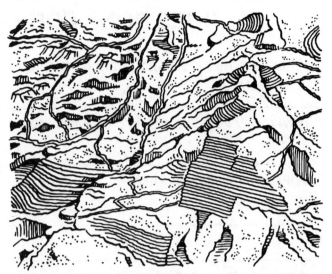

The potato was the most important food of the Incas. They called it *papa.* The Incas had many varieties and colors of potatoes, and today we know of 40 of those varieties. The potato became the main source of food for the Incas since they could plant it at great heights

Using step-like terraces carved into the mountain sides, the Incas created more flat land for crops. The terraces, which are still used today, also helped control soil erosion.

in the Andes Mountains. Some of the varieties of potato would also resist the frosts of the region.

The Incas used the first known freeze-dried process. They left the potatoes outside to freeze. Then the Incas trampled the potatoes by foot to squeeze the water out of them. Next they left them in the sunlight to dry. The Incas called these dried potatoes *chuñu.* The Incas preserved chuñu either whole or ground into flour. Chuñu would last for years without spoiling and was easy to store. The Incas were able to eat it throughout the year.

Corn was another important Incan crop. The Incas planted over 20 varieties of corn. Corn is called maize by many Indian tribes. The Incas named it *sara.* Corn was grown only in the lower regions.

The mountains presented farmers with special challenges. To create enough flat land for the crops, the Incas carved flat step-like terraces into the mountain sides. The terraces also helped to keep the soil from being eroded. Modern Andes farmers still use many of the ancient Incan terraces.

Planting the crops was a group effort. The men would break up the soil with planting sticks. The women then followed, putting the seeds into the earth. The children often worked in the fields to scare away birds and animals that might eat the crops before the harvest.

The Incas also developed a system to carry the water of the mountain streams to the terraces. They dug canals and tunnels and built raised aqueducts to carry the water. The Incan water system is still in use today.

Farming was the subject of many Incan religious ceremonies. After the planting season, the Incas made sacrifices to the rain god. At another major festival, the Incas thanked the gods for a good harvest.

Name _____ Date _____

QUESTIONS FOR CONSIDERATION

1. What was the most important food to the ancient Incas?

_____

2. How many varieties of this crop were there?

_____

3. Why was this food popular?

_____

_____

4. What was the Incan name for corn?

_____

5. What were Incan "freeze dried" potatoes called?

_____

6. How did the Incas make more flat farm land?

_____

_____

7. How did Incas irrigate their farm land?

_____

_____

8. What in the text might make you believe that the Incas designed things to last?

_____

_____

9. Why might farming be the subject of religious ceremonies?

_____

_____

10. When did Incas sacrifice to the rain god?

_____

_____

Name _____ Date _____

INCAN AGRICULTURE—WORD SEARCH

Find and circle the names of the Incan foods listed in the puzzle. The words may be placed horizontally, vertically, or diagonally. They may be spelled forward or backward.

WORD LIST

AVOCADOS	CORN	POTATOES
BEANS	PEPPERS	SQUASH
CASHEWS	PEANUTS	STRAWBERRIES
CHOCOLATE	PINEAPPLE	TOMATOES
CHUÑU	PAPA	SARA

```
S  I  U  V  U  K  A  F  S  L  N  X  R  R  T  C  N  I  N  J
S  Q  S  N  O  X  H  R  W  Y  M  Y  Y  B  L  K  T  O  P  P
P  M  O  A  Y  S  T  R  E  W  M  F  D  T  M  L  X  P  G  B
D  C  Z  K  R  D  Q  S  H  G  H  A  E  H  J  C  S  M  Z  Z
Y  P  Z  T  J  A  D  R  S  G  C  H  O  C  O  L  A  T  E  K
C  T  I  X  U  Q  Y  J  A  H  O  I  F  N  N  P  T  O  N  G
D  X  S  N  M  T  S  Y  C  Y  K  E  H  I  E  X  Q  U  S  O
A  X  E  W  E  H  F  T  N  L  S  O  D  A  C  O  V  A  C  D
B  N  I  V  L  A  D  A  N  V  B  B  S  S  W  P  J  C  Y  J
V  T  R  P  U  L  P  B  Z  P  E  A  K  E  T  K  X  C  R  V
G  F  R  I  N  M  F  P  C  Q  A  R  N  B  O  U  S  O  I  F
K  I  E  L  U  U  P  R  L  M  N  D  W  M  I  T  N  N  G  Q
G  P  B  S  H  K  S  L  J  E  S  X  D  Y  T  A  A  A  B  L
A  B  W  N  C  U  P  E  H  R  D  P  X  P  O  C  N  T  E  S
C  G  A  V  P  N  A  G  S  E  M  S  J  E  M  E  O  A  O  P
T  K  R  G  Y  H  P  J  A  E  Y  S  P  P  A  X  D  R  X  P
D  K  T  C  T  D  A  H  U  F  G  H  J  P  T  Q  U  I  N  J
X  U  S  R  C  O  Z  L  Q  I  X  B  S  E  O  J  T  S  A  G
X  P  K  Z  D  M  B  V  S  O  Y  J  J  R  E  P  E  E  O  V
O  S  R  T  X  Z  J  R  I  X  D  D  M  S  S  D  Z  V  C  E
```

INCAN WEAVING

Weaving was one of the most important crafts of the ancient Incas. The women did most of the dying, spinning, and weaving of cloth. However many Incan men were also weavers.

The Incas used wool for weaving most of their cloth. Llama wool is very coarse and is varied in color. The Incas used it to make blankets and ropes. Wool from the alpaca is white with some gray and brown. The Incas used alpaca wool to weave clothing. The wool from the vicuña is a soft fiber. They used vicuña wool for weaving the finest cloth. When the Spanish invaders first saw cloth woven from vicuña wool, they thought it was silk.

One type of loom used by Incan women was the backstrap loom.

Cotton could not be grown in the mountain regions of the Incas. When the Incan empire spread to the coast, cotton became available through trade with other tribes and soon became popular with the Incan weavers.

Three types of looms were used by Incan weavers. The most unusual was the backstrap loom. They tied one end of the loom to a tree. They then tied the other end to a belt that went around the weaver's back. The Incas also used a horizontal loom. It was stretched about a foot off the ground between wooden supports. They also used a vertical loom, attached to a wall. The weaver using this loom would stand to work.

Incan cloth had bright, bold colors. They obtained the colors to dye the wool from many sources. They used metals such as copper and tin for some of the dyes. The Incas also used vegetable dyes. The indigo plant gave a bright blue dye, and the achiote tree was the source of a brilliant red dye. A dye made from ground shellfish provided a deep purple color.

Several steps were necessary in the production of wool cloth. The Incas gathered the wool from the animals. The women then dyed the wool. After drying it, they spun the wool into thread. Next, they wove the thread into cloth. The Incan weavers used geometric patterns. Seldom did a weaver repeat the same pattern.

The Incas used embroidery to decorate some of the cloth. Some of the better garments had decorations of gold, silver, or copper attached to them, and some garments had feathers woven into them for extra color and decoration.

A group of women called the "chosen women" lived in the temples. They wove the finest wool into garments for the ruler. He only wore each garment once, and then it was destroyed.

Today, descendants of the ancient Incas still weave beautiful, bright textiles. The methods and designs used have remained unchanged for about 3,000 years.

Name _____ Date _____

QUESTIONS FOR CONSIDERATION

1. Name three animals the Incas used as sources of wool.

_____

_____

2. What did they use to make blankets and rope?

_____

3. What was alcapa used for?

_____

4. What did the Spanish think the finest wool cloth really was?

_____

5. What item became popular as the Incan empire grew?

_____

6. What type of loom that was used by the Incas was most unusual?

_____

7. What types of minerals were used as sources of dye colors?

_____

8. What color was obtained from the indigo plant?

_____

9. From what did the Incas get purple dye?

_____

10. What did the "chosen women" do?

_____

_____

Name _____ Date _____

INCAN WEAVING—CROSSWORD

Use the clues below to complete the crossword puzzle.

ACROSS

3. Metal and_____ dyes were used to color the cloth.
6. Wool from this animal is white with some gray and brown.
12. The Incan weavers used this type of pattern.
13. This plant is used to make a bright blue dye.
14. This wool was used to make the finest cloth.
15. _____ women wove garments for the ruler.

DOWN

1. The Incas used _____, bold colors.
2. The Incas traded for_____ with other tribes.
4. This animal provided a very course wool that the Incas used to make blankets.
5. This type of Incan loom was fastened around the weaver's back.
7. This animal is ground to make a deep purple color.
8. This type of Incan loom was stretched about a foot off the ground.
9. This type of Incan loom was attached to a wall.
10. The craft of making fiber threads into cloth
11. Source of a brilliant red dye

56

INCAN ARTS AND CRAFTS

The Incas are most famous for their weaving, but they also developed skills in metalwork. They used gold, silver, copper, and tin. They discovered how to make bronze by melting copper and tin together. Incan men mined the precious metals. They did not use slaves to work in the mines. Instead, the Incas did this work as part of their "work tax." The Incas had to give a certain amount of their labor to the government.

All of the gold became the property of the ruler. Metal workers pounded much of the gold into thin sheets to

Even though Incan pottery was made for practical use, the pieces were decorated with elaborate geometric patterns.

cover the walls of the palaces. They also made statues and other decorations for the ruler. The ruler and nobles also used silver for decoration. They believed that silver was the metal of the Moon. Craftsmen also used gold and silver to make masks, plates, and jewelry.

Spanish invaders reported seeing life-size statues made of bronze and covered in gold. After the conquests of the Incas, the Spaniards melted down most of the Incan gold and shipped it to Spain. Very few Incan artworks made of gold still exist.

Copper, tin, and bronze were also used to make artistic, as well as useful, items. Archaeologists have found many examples of Incan metal items such as knives, weapons, pins for garments, and tools.

The Incas also created a variety of pottery. Examples survive of three-legged pots, plates, and drinking cups. The most unusual Incan pottery was the aryballuses. This was a jar with a pointed bottom. It balanced itself upright when filled. It rested on its side when empty. Much of Incan pottery had knobs attached to it to which ropes could be tied for carrying it.

The Incas made most of their pottery for use rather than art. Even so, it was beautiful. Their pottery is know for its elaborate yet small geometric patterns.

The Incas also had a special method of applying colors to the pottery. However, the secret of the ancient Incan method of coloring pottery is lost. Most Incan pottery was red, white, and black. At times they also used yellow and orange.

The crafts of weaving, metal work, and pottery are still being done by the descendants of the ancient Incas. They still use many of the same methods and designs of their ancestors.

Name _____ Date _____

QUESTIONS FOR CONSIDERATION

1. What metal did the Incas produce by mixing copper and tin together?

_____

2. What type of tax was placed on Incas by their government?

_____

3. What metal automatically became the property of the ruler when it was mined?

_____

4. What did the Incas believe about silver?

_____

5. What did the invaders do with the Incan gold?

_____

_____

6. Why did Incan pottery have knobs on it?

_____

_____

7. What was an aryballuses?

_____

_____

8. How did Incas color their pottery?

_____

_____

9. What colors were used on Incan pottery?

_____

10. Do any Incan descendants still do Incan crafts? If so, what crafts do they do?

_____

_____

Name _____ Date _____

INCAN ARTS AND CRAFTS—WORD SCRAMBLE

Unscramble the following groups of letters to form words that were used in the chapter on Incan Arts and Crafts:

1. givewan _____

2. wtokmaler _____

3. zenrob _____

4. susatte _____

5. levirs _____

6. torypet _____

7. ssaallburey _____

8. migoretce _____

9. norage _____

10. nessdig _____

11. wereljy _____

12. ercpop _____

13. ipnaS _____

14. soknb _____

15. ooctaeidnrs _____

INCAN ROADS AND BRIDGES

The Incas built one of the ancient world's best transportation systems. They built roads and bridges to keep the empire together. The transportation system allowed them to have fast communication between villages and cities. They also used it to move food and other supplies. The roads also allowed military troops to move faster.

The Incan roads stretched for more than 10,000 miles. The Incas had two major roads. The Royal Road was 3,250 miles long. It went from the northern border of the empire through Ecuador, Peru, and Bolivia into Argentina and Chile.

The other major road, the coastal highway, was 2,520 miles long.

The Apurimac Chaca, the hanging bridge over the Apurimac River in Peru, was one of the most famous of the Incan chacas. It is known as The Bridge of San Luis Rey in literature.

It ran from the village of Tumbes in the north, through the desert, then into Chile.

Several other roads ran between the two major ones. The standard width of the roads was 24 feet. They were narrower only when natural barriers were in the way. The roads included side walls to keep out sand drifts and to mark the road. There were also markers along the road to tell the distance to the next village.

Incan workers provided the labor to build the roads as part of the "labor tax" they paid to the government. Government engineers directed the workers.

The roads belonged to the government. No one could use the road without special permission. The Incas did not use wheeled vehicles on their roads. The travelers and messengers walked to their destinations. The Incas used llamas to carry goods on the roads. They built rest houses called *tampus* about every 12 to 20 miles along the roads. In addition to providing a place to rest, most tampus also had food available.

The Incas built causeways to elevate the roads in swampy areas. They also built amazing bridges, which they called *chacas.* The hanging bridges are the most famous of the Incan chacas. One Incan bridge was over 250 feet long. Built in 1350, it lasted until 1890.

The Incas used the fibers of the maguey plant to weave the cable for the bridges. The main cables were from four to five feet thick. Incan workers had to replace the cables about every two years.

The Incas also built pontoon bridges made of reed boats tied together. Another type of Incan bridge had a basket hung from a cable stretched between two stone towers. Travelers got into the basket, and a workman then pulled along the cable to the other side.

Name _____ Date _____

QUESTIONS FOR CONSIDERATION

1. How many miles of Incan roads were there?

_____

2. What was the longest Incan road called?

_____

3. What was the name of the other major Incan road?

_____

4. How wide were most Incan roads?

_____

5. What kind of walls did the roads have? Why?

_____

_____

6. What were Incan rest houses called?

_____

7. What was a chaca?

_____

_____

8. What plant fibers did the Incas weave together to make cables for their bridges?

_____

9. Of what were pontoon bridge boats made?

_____

10. Describe another type of Incan bridge.

_____

_____

Name _____ Date _____

INCAN ROADS AND BRIDGES—WORD SEARCH

Find and circle the following words in the puzzle. The words may be placed horizontally, vertically, or diagonally. They may be spelled forward or backward.

WORD LIST

BRIDGES	MAGUEY	TAMPUS	CAUSEWAYS
PONTOON	TRAVELERS	CHACAS	ROYAL ROAD
VEHICLES	REEDS	SUSPENSION	BASKETS
TOWERS	SIDE WALLS	CABLES	WALK
TRANSPORTATION		LLAMAS	LABOR TAX
COASTAL HIGHWAY			

```
U  R  M  A  S  T  R  Q  O  T  A  M  P  U  S  M  R  R  J  H
X  F  D  B  A  E  A  Q  W  X  J  A  K  K  K  I  C  N  V  M
Z  S  C  C  A  B  L  V  N  V  A  U  U  K  I  H  V  J  C  R
I  D  O  D  V  S  T  B  R  J  X  T  I  S  A  Y  W  E  K  J
R  A  A  Q  Q  V  K  R  A  G  D  L  R  C  A  V  S  G  Y  O
V  O  S  Q  T  N  R  E  A  C  T  S  A  O  Y  M  Q  C  M  B
T  R  T  G  L  M  B  I  T  N  P  S  Y  T  B  R  A  K  N  O
W  L  A  S  I  A  M  S  V  S  S  N  Q  A  T  A  G  L  A  Y
N  A  L  U  H  G  V  Q  K  M  C  P  L  L  W  V  L  N  L  U
O  Y  H  S  X  U  N  B  L  M  M  Q  O  U  H  E  G  B  Z  G
O  O  I  P  E  E  I  F  A  K  N  X  B  R  Q  K  S  K  G  M
T  R  G  E  G  Y  Z  N  W  A  C  G  H  Z  T  B  O  U  F  C
N  H  H  N  N  K  B  S  P  U  V  I  R  D  S  A  X  F  A  T
O  F  W  S  T  R  A  V  E  L  E  R  S  Z  T  A  T  K  H  C
P  Y  A  I  T  I  G  R  B  G  N  I  C  D  O  Z  M  I  G  F
G  Z  Y  O  M  O  E  D  I  P  D  F  J  Z  W  S  L  D  O  M
V  W  L  N  S  L  L  A  W  E  D  I  S  K  E  H  D  R  U  N
A  B  V  U  U  V  M  U  S  E  P  B  R  G  R  B  A  E  R  X
P  H  V  E  R  Y  S  Q  W  Q  E  L  M  B  S  U  L  W  E  Y
V  E  H  I  C  L  E  S  W  I  L  E  R  V  C  A  S  Y  K  R
```

CITIES OF THE INCAS

The Incas were master builders. They had the best planned cities in the ancient Americas. Planners laid out the cities in a grid. Each city had a central plaza, with the major temples and public buildings surrounding it. The center of each city included temples, a palace for the visiting Inca, and housing for the priests and nobles. Houses for the common people surrounded the central area.

Incan architects used trapezoidal openings for the doors and windows in their buildings. The buildings were made of huge cut and polished stones set perfectly in place.

A wall that was 50 feet high encircled the city of Chimu. However, most Incan cities did not have walls around them. The Incas built large stone fortresses near the city. The citizens would gather inside the fortress in time of danger.

Incan buildings remain among the most amazing ever built. The Incas used huge blocks of stone. One stone measured 36 x 18 x 6 feet. They cut and polished each stone with small stone tools and then moved each stone into the proper place. The stones fit together perfectly, so the builders did not need to use cement to keep them in place. Even today, a knife blade cannot fit into the cracks between the stones of the ancient buildings.

The Incas used trapezoidal openings for all of their doors and windows. The four-sided openings were smaller at the top than at the bottom. The Incas did not decorate the outside of their buildings, but they made beautiful decorations for the insides of the palaces and temples. They often used solid gold for these decorations.

The two most famous Incan cities are Cuzco and Machu Picchu. Incan legend says that the first Incan ruler founded Cuzco. This happened in about A.D. 1100. Cuzco soon became capital of the entire empire. It is in a mountain valley about 11,000 feet above sea level. Two rivers flowed into the valley to supply water.

Wars and invaders destroyed the ancient city. In 1400 Cuzco was rebuilt. The new city had two large plazas, the Inca's palace, the Sun Temple, and other temples and government buildings.

The best preserved Incan city is Machu Picchu. Explorers rediscovered it in 1911. Its ruins include temples, palaces, military buildings, and common houses. The Incas of Machu Picchu built terraces for farming. They also had a stone aqueduct to bring in water from a mile away.

Name _____ Date _____

QUESTIONS FOR CONSIDERATION

1. What did each city have?

_____

_____

2. What did the Incas build near each city?

_____

3. What did Incas do when they built buildings that was so unusual?

_____

_____

4. What was the shape of Incan doors and windows?

_____

5. How did Incas decorate the insides of their major buildings?

_____

_____

6. What was the capital of the Incan empire?

_____

7. When was the capital built?

_____

8. What is the name of the best-preserved Incan city?

_____

9. When did explorers discover the best-preserved Incan city?

_____

10. What did the Incas of Machu Picchu make to aid farming?

_____

_____

Name _____ Date _____

CITIES OF THE INCAS—CROSSWORD

Use the clues below to complete the crossword puzzle.

ACROSS

1. All Incan cities had at least one of these large, open-air squares.
4. Machu Picchu was _____ in 1911.
8. Solid _____ was often used for decoration.
9. Every Incan city had this building used to worship a god or goddess.
12. Incan citizens would gather inside this structure in times of danger.
14. This is the best preserved ancient Incan city.

DOWN

1. The ruler of the city lived in this building.
2. Incan cities were laid out in a _____.
3. Buildings were made of cut and polished _____.
5. Cuzco was the _____ of the Incan empire.
6. This is used to bring water across land.
7. The Incas often built one of these to give them more farmland.
10. The Incas used this shape for all of their doors and windows.
11. According to legend, this city was founded by the first Inca.
13. This Incan city was surrounded by a 50-foot high wall.

THE INCA AND HIS GOVERNMENT

Inca was the title of the ruler of the Incan empire. At first, the word "Inca" meant the children of the sun god Inti. It later became the title of the ruler. Today, we also use Inca to mean the people of the tribe.

The ancient Incas believed their ruler was a descendant of the gods. They worshiped him as both a god and a ruler, and he had absolute power.

The Inca had many wives. His main wife was his queen. Her title was *coya.* The Inca's sister could also be his coya. The Inca might have over 100 children. The oldest son of the Inca did not automatically become the

The Inca and his main wife, the coya, were carried in a golden litter by servants.

next ruler; instead, a council of nobles chose the next ruler. Usually, the council chose the most promising son of the coya. At times the selection of the new Inca led to fighting among the supporters of various sons.

A *borla,* or Incan crown, was worn by the Inca. It had a fringe of brightly colored cords. Gold tubes decorated the end of each cord. The Inca wore garments of the finest wool. Each of his garments was worn only once. The Inca ate and drank only from gold plates and goblets.

Servants carried the Inca on a platform and chair made of gold since he didn't walk great distances. The chair, called a litter, had a canopy of gold and jewels to protect the Inca from rain and the rays of the Sun.

Each Inca had a new palace built. The walls of the Inca's palace were decorated with gold. The Inca's throne was also gold.

The empire had a 30-day period of mourning after the death of the Inca. Priests mummified the Inca's body. Many of the Inca's servants volunteered to die, because they believed that they would then be able to continue to serve the Inca. The old palace became a shrine for the previous Inca. They put the Inca's mummified body into the shrine, and the people then worshiped the mummies of the Incas.

The Incas had an efficient government. The rulers, priests, and generals all came from the noble class. Most were relatives of the Inca. The Inca used the road and bridge system to help him govern. Messengers and soldiers were able to move quickly throughout the empire.

All Incan men gave the government physical labor. This was the *mita,* or service tax. The government built the great palaces, public buildings, and roads with this labor.

66

Name _____ Date _____

QUESTIONS FOR CONSIDERATION

1. What was the title of the ruler of the Incan empire?

_____

2. Why did the people worship their ruler?

_____

3. What was the title of the Incan queen?

_____

4. How was a new ruler chosen?

_____

_____

5. What was the royal crown called? Describe it.

_____

_____

6. How did the ruler travel?

_____

7. What did each new ruler have? Why?

_____

_____

8. How were dead rulers remembered?

_____

_____

9. What was the name of the Incan capital?

_____

10. What was a mita?

_____

_____

Name _____ Date _____

THE INCA AND HIS GOVERNMENT—WORD SCRAMBLE

Unscramble the following groups of letters to form words that were used in the chapter on the Incan and his government.

1. nadnedcet _____

2. yoca _____

3. lonciuc fo slboen _____

4. arlob _____

5. tilret _____

6. coypan _____

7. cealap _____

8. smemimu _____

9. ouzCc _____

10. tima _____

11. tiln _____

12. onrcw _____

13. henris _____

14. lasoeutb oerpw _____

15. pmreei _____

THE LLAMA: THE ANIMAL OF THE INCAS

The llama was used as a pack animal by the Incas, and it was also a source of wool, leather, and meat.

The most important animal to the Incas was the llama. It was the only large native animal of the Western Hemisphere to be tamed. The horse and cow came to the Americas later. The Incas were the only people of South or Central America to use animals to help in their work.

The llama is a member of the camel family. It is about four feet tall at its shoulder and about four feet long plus a tail of about six inches. An adult llama can weigh up to 300 pounds. The llama has a slender body, long neck, and long thin legs. Its head is similar to that of a camel. It has large eyes and a pointed snout with a split nose. Its hooves have two toes.

Although the llama does not have a hump like its cousin the camel, its body stores water well. The llama can travel great distances without needing water.

The Incas used llamas to carry food and trading goods throughout the empire. The animal is well suited to the rugged mountains of the Andes. It also adapts well to high altitudes. The llama can carry loads of about 100 to 130 pounds and can easily travel six to 12 miles per day over uneven ground. On flat ground it can travel 20 to 25 miles in one day. The llama can even run faster than a horse when necessary.

The llama was, and still is, a source of wool. Its wool is thick and greasy and comes in a variety of colors. The Incas used llama wool to make blankets, ropes, and sacks to carry goods. They tanned the hide of the llama to make leather. Many Incas used this leather to make sandals.

The llama was also a source of food. The Incas dried llama meat in the heat of the Sun. *Charqui* is the Incan name for dried llama meat. Our word "jerky" comes from the Incan word charqui.

Today the llama is still an important animal in the Andes Mountains. The descendants of the ancient Incas use the llama in much the same way as their ancestors did.

Name _____ Date _____

QUESTIONS FOR CONSIDERATION

1. What was the only large animal native to the Western Hemisphere to be tamed?

_____

2. What animal is the llama related to?

_____

3. How much can an adult llama weigh?

_____

4. Why is the llama a good animal to have in the Andes Mountains?

_____

_____

5. How much can a llama carry?

_____

6. How fast can a llama run?

_____

7. What is llama wool good for?

_____

_____

8. What is llama leather good for?

_____

_____

9. What is charqui?

_____

_____

10. How are llamas useful today?

_____

_____

Name _____ Date _____

THE LLAMA—WORD SEARCH

Find and circle the following words in the puzzle. The words may be placed horizontally, vertically, or diagonally. They may be spelled forward or backward.

WORD LIST

ANDES	HIDE	MOUNTAINS	CAMEL
JERKY	POINTED SNOUT	WESTERN	HEMISPHERE
WOOL	WATER	LLAMA	CHARQUI
HORSE	ROPES	BLANKETS	NATIVE ANIMAL
SANDALS	SLENDER BODY	HIGH ALTITUDES	LEATHER

```
F P H J X L Q K B A F E S V V Z R E B S
K M D I K H A Y X C L N H C V E S E E T
V A O D G P Z M Y L V L J R T E C S R E
O S D U A H L H I P A T N A K N C L F K
G N S I N B A E Z N E U W P F F A E R N
I M C A M T Z L O K A T Z F P D D N F A
U M C J N Q A S T E L E Q M O Q I D S L
B F C A N D L I S I F W V U I N N E E B
U I N F V B A R N L T A N I N S S R E R
B Z F S W A O L E S W U N Z T I I B Y D
L R S C J H E B S X M R D J E A T O K L
S E P O R P Q R J Y E N O E D A N D R H
O T A A D H D K E T Z M X W S N L Y E C
S E A T O J J K S H V C N O N F N F J X
G E Q B H J L E A V P H O O O Q L O L V
B D D V C E W P I M X S I L U X U T L L
A L I N I M R D U O O L I D T J H S A K
W Z E T A H A N Z N G O N M E O G L M G
Y F P L K S R I C A M E L N E U B S A I
N I I U Q R A H C M C D X E X H Y O C P
```

71

THE INCAS AND THE SPANISH CONQUEST

The Incas had little contact with the Mayas or the Aztecs. They did not know of the earliest arrival of the white man, nor did they know of the Spanish conquest of the other tribes.

The Incan ruler, Huyayna Capac, died in 1525. He did not choose an heir to become the new ruler. Two of his sons, Atahualpa and Huscar, fought each other for this honor. Their fighting caused a bloody civil war that lasted for over five years. Atahualpa won the war and became the next ruler. He then ordered the death of thousands of Huscar's soldiers and his family.

After agreeing to meet with the Spanish, Atahualpa was ambushed by Pizarro and his men. Atahualpa paid a huge ransom in gold and silver, but the Spanish executed him anyway.

The Incas soon received reports of strange-looking pale men with beards. An enemy tribe of the Incas captured a shipwrecked European on the coast of Brazil. He joined the enemies in some fighting against the Incas. He was the first white man that the Incas ever saw. The Incas also heard stories of white men arriving in giant boats.

The Spanish landed on the Caribbean coast on May 13, 1532. Over 180 Spanish soldiers arrived to search for gold. Led by Francisco Pizarro, they brought with them guns, armor, a cannon, and horses. This was the first time that horses appeared in the new world. These strange new animals fascinated and frightened the Incas.

Atahualpa and Pizarro agreed to meet in a courtyard in the town of Cajamarca. Atahualpa and his men arrived without weapons. The Incas believed the Spanish might be gods, and so they did not want to offend the Spanish by being armed.

The Spanish, however, had planned an ambush. Atahualpa arrived in the courtyard carried on a gold throne. The Spanish then opened fire. They soon killed over 2,000 Incas. The Spanish captured Atahualpa and put him in a prison. Atahualpa agreed to pay the Spanish a ransom of enough gold and silver to fill his prison cell.

Even after he paid the ransom, the Spanish refused to free Atahualpa. They condemned Atahualpa to death and gave him a choice: would he prefer that they strangle him or burn him at the stake? He chose strangulation. With Atahualpa's death, the great Incan empire came under Spanish rule and influence.

72

Name _____ Date _____

QUESTIONS FOR CONSIDERATION

1. Why didn't the Incas know about the Spanish conquest of other tribes?

_____

_____

2. Why was there a civil war among the Incas?

_____

_____

3. How long did the civil war last?

_____

4. Who won the civil war?

_____

5. Who was the first white man ever seen by the Incas?

_____

6. When did the Spanish land on the Caribbean coast?

_____

7. Who was the leader of the Spanish?

_____

8. What did the Spanish bring with them that frightened the Incas?

_____

9. Why did the Incas meet the Spanish unarmed?

_____

_____

10. What did the Incan ruler fill with gold and silver?

_____

_____

Name _____ Date _____

THE INCAS AND THE SPANISH CONQUEST CROSSWORD

Use the clues below to complete the crossword puzzle.

ACROSS

1. The Incas had little contact with the Mayas or _____.
4. Where the first European the Incas met was ship-wrecked
8. The Incan ruler paid this to the Spanish.
9. The last great ruler of the Incan empire
11. At first, the Incas thought the Spanish were these.
12. A native of Europe
13. The nationality of the victors over the Incas.
15. The Incan ruler and his soldiers were ambushed here.

DOWN

2. How Atahualpa died
3. The Spanish came to the new world in search of _____.
5. The Incas did not have these when they met the Spanish in the town of Cajamarca.
6. The Spanish leader's last name
7. The Spanish brought this animal to the new world for the first time.
10. This son of the Inca lost his fight with his brother.
14. The Spaniards put the Incan ruler into this.

74

THE AZTECS

The Aztec capital, Tenochtitlan, was built on an island in the Lake Texcoco.

The Aztec Indians had already built one of the most advanced civilizations in the western hemisphere by the time Columbus made his first voyage to the Americas. Archaeologists believe that the Aztec capital Tenochtitlan may have had a population of over 200,000. This was larger than any city in Spain or England during the same time.

Mythology tells that the Aztecs began as wandering tribes in the north or northwest part of Mexico. This territory, called Aztlan, is the source of the name Aztec. Today we refer to the people as Aztecs, but they called themselves Mexica or Tenochca.

The ancient tribes wandered for many years. In the 1200s they began to settle in the Valley of Mexico, which is in the central part of the country. The area rises about 7,500 feet above sea level. It is surround by tropical rain forests, but the high altitude gave the region a mild climate.

Nahuatl was the language spoken by the Aztecs. Many words we use today came from this ancient language. Aztec words include Acapulco, Mexico, avocado, chocolate, and tomato. The Aztecs developed a form of picture writing. Some pictures represented ideas; other pictures stood for sounds. They did not develop an alphabet, so their writing was limited in what it could express.

The Aztecs soon founded their greatest city, Tenochtitlan, on an island in the Lake Texcoco. This is the site of the Mexico City, the modern capital of Mexico.

By the early 1400s, the Aztecs had gained control of their region and established a number of city-states. Each city-state had its own government and distinct culture. The three major city-states—Tenochtitlan, Texaco, and Tlatelolco—formed an alliance that became the Aztec empire. At one time 489 cities paid tribute and taxes to the empire.

A council of nobles always chose the emperor from members of the royal family. The greatest emperor, Montezuma I, ruled from 1440 to 1468/9. His name is also spelled Moctezuma and Motecuhzoma. He expanded the empire from the Atlantic to Pacific coasts and from Central America to what is now Guatemala. His grandson, Montezuma II, became emperor in 1502. He ruled when the empire was at its peak.

The Aztecs made no attempt to unify the area they commanded or to change the customs of the conquered peoples. The emperor stationed military units throughout the empire to maintain control. A great noble commanded each army and also served as governor. Most offices were hereditary, but service to the emperor was also a way to obtain a high office.

Aztecs belonged to a large family group called a *calpolli,* a word that meant "big house." Each calpolli owned a plot of land to meet the needs of its members. In addition to providing necessities for their own members, each calpolli presented the government with part of the harvest as a tribute.

There were four main social classes in Aztec society. The upper-class nobles owned land in addition to the land of their calpolli. The commoners farmed the calpolli land or made crafts and gave tributes to the nobles in return for protection. Serfs who farmed land of the nobles formed the third major class. Slaves were the lowest class. They had either been captives in war, criminals, or citizens who became unable to pay their debts. Slaves became household servants or worked alongside the serfs in the fields.

Spaniards, under the leadership of Hernando Cortés, invaded Mexico in search of gold. Many of the smaller city-states helped the Spanish destroy the Aztec empire in 1521. They helped the Spanish because they resented paying tributes to the Aztec empire.

The glory of the Aztec empire vanished during the Spanish invasion, but today Aztec designs still have a strong influence on Mexican art, and thousands of modern Mexicans can trace their ancestry to the Aztecs.

Name _____ Date _____

QUESTIONS FOR CONSIDERATION

1. Where does the word Aztec come from?

_____

_____

2. Where did the Aztecs settle in the 1200s?

_____

3. What was the name of the Aztec capital?

_____

4. What is located where the Aztec capital once was?

_____

5. What was the language of the Aztecs known as?

_____

6. What type of writing did the Aztecs use?

_____

_____

7. Who was the greatest Aztec emperor?

_____

8. What was an Aztec family group called?

_____

9. Why did the Spanish invade Mexico?

_____

_____

10. Who was the leader of the Spanish invasion?

_____

Name _____ Date _____

THE AZTECS—MAPPING IT OUT

Using a map or atlas to help you, write the name of the following places in the proper locations on the map.

Baja California
Balsas River
Gulf of Mexico
Mexico City (This was the location of the ancient Aztec city of Tenochtitlan)
Pacific Ocean
Rio Grande
Sierra Madre Mountains
Yucatan Peninsula

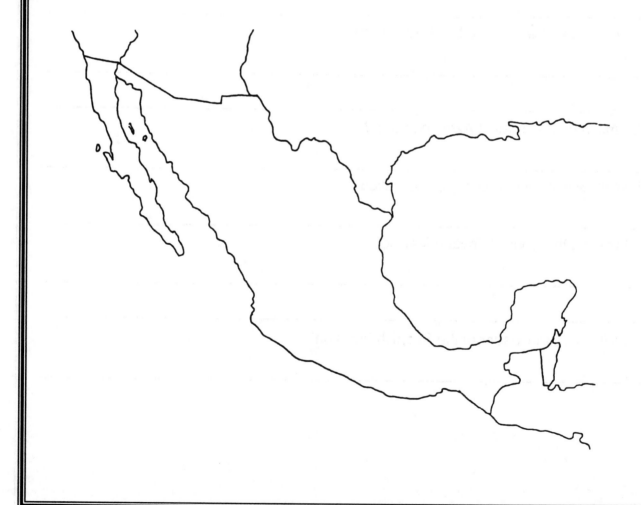

AZTEC DAILY LIFE

Huetzin woke up an hour before the Sun appeared. He rolled his sleeping mat into a small bundle and put it into the corner of the room. He was still sleepy as he went into the small steam bath attached to his house. He threw some water onto the hot rocks to make the steam. As the steam subsided, he went outside and dove into the canal that ran along beside the house. He shivered at the cold water of the canal. Now he was fully awake.

Aztec women baked cornmeal pancakes (tortillas) twice a day in the kitchen areas of their houses.

A small house made of adobe brick was home to Huetzin. The house had a roof made of thatched straw. Aztec homes had little furniture. They used woven straw mats that were placed on the dirt floors instead of beds and chairs. The only pieces of furniture Huetzin's family owned were a few wooden chests to hold valuables and kitchen utensils.

Some of the houses were large because many family members lived together. Households included the husband and wife and their unmarried children, as well as other relatives of the husband. The rooms of the house surrounded a patio. The kitchen and eating area was the largest room in the house. The fire was in the middle of the room. Each morning Huetzin's mother would rekindle the fire and begin her chores of preparing the family's food for the day. She packed a special lunch for Huetzin and his father to eat at the workshop. Huetzin had a pouch filled with food just like the one his father carried. Huetzin carried his own lunch to the workshop. Aztecs expected the children to share in all of the work.

Most of Huetzin's relatives were farmers in the nearby fields, but his father was a craftsman. His father carved jade and other precious stones into small decorations. Every day Huetzin would go to the workshop with his father. His father taught him many things. He learned how to hunt and fish as well as how to use the tools to create beautiful objects to be sold in the market. He also learned the stories of his ancestors from his father.

Huetzin looked forward to his next birthday. Then he could attend the Telpuchcalli. This was a school sponsored by his family's tribe. Both boys and girls attended the Aztec schools. Training at the school included lessons in citizenship, history and tradition, religious ceremonies, and arts and crafts. In addition to these classes, the boys learned about methods of warfare. The girls learned singing and dancing skills. Some students also went to the Calmecac, which was a special school to train priests.

All of the children helped with the household chores. Huetzin's sisters remained at home with their mother. The girls learned cooking, spinning cotton, weaving, and other household skills. The women of the household prepared the meals and made the clothing for the family.

Huetzin and his family wore cotton clothes with some decoration sewn on. His family was wealthy enough to afford cotton. The poorer Aztecs wore cloth made of fibers of the maguey plant. Decoration on clothing indicated the wealth and social rank of the person. Members of the upper class wore colorful and highly embroidered clothing.

Men wore a loincloth wrapped around their hips. Some men also wore cloaks tied over one shoulder. Aztec women wore loose, sleeveless blouses and wraparound skirts. People went barefoot most of the time, but some wore sandals made of leather or woven maguey fibers.

All day, Huetzin helped his father at the workshop. He looked forward to the time when he would be a master stone carver and work alongside his father. He and his father ate lunch with the others at the workshop. That afternoon Huetzin went to the marketplace and helped sell the carvings that had been made during the week.

Huetzin and his father returned home just before sunset. They washed in the canal and then joined the rest of the family for supper. The women served the meal to the men of the household and then ate their own meals separately.

The Aztecs had a variety of food available. Members of the family brought maize (corn), beans, squash, chili peppers, and tomatoes from the fields. The men hunted to provide deer, rabbits, ducks, and geese. The Aztecs raised dogs and turkeys for additional meat.

Corn was the main part of the Aztec diet. Twice daily, the women baked the cornmeal pancake, which the Spanish later called a tortilla. The Aztecs filled the tortillas with other foods much like our tamales and tacos today.

The Aztecs did not have cattle or pigs so they had little fat in their diets. The food was baked or boiled. Since they used many peppers in their cooking, the food was often spicy and hot.

Two special treats at the end of the meal might include chicle-zapoil or chocolate. Chicle came from a gum tree and is the basis for modern-day chewing gum. Chocolate was processed from the cacao bean. It was a delicacy and not served often. Many times the Aztecs flavored their chocolate with vanilla and other spices.

After the meal, all members of the family worked on various chores. Huetzin's father mended tools for tomorrow's work. His uncle repaired a broken planting stick. The women continued working at their looms.

This was Huetzin's favorite part of the day. As they worked in the dim glow of the fire, Huetzin listened to his grandfather tell stories of battles of the old days. Grandfather seemed to like the old days. Huetzin knew many of the stories by heart, but he enjoyed hearing his grandfather tell them again.

Soon it was time for Huetzin to go to bed. He went to his room and unrolled his sleeping mat. He was tired from his busy day, and it was not long before he fell asleep.

Name _____ Date _____

QUESTIONS FOR CONSIDERATION

1. What in America is similar to the Aztec steam bath?

_____

2. What was the name of the Aztec schools?

_____

3. Who could attend them?

_____

4. Describe the typical dress for an Aztec man.

_____

_____

5. What did Aztecs use to make clothing?

_____

6. What Aztec food, if any, would you enjoy eating?

_____

7. What Aztec food, if any, would you not want to eat?

_____

Match the following words with the correct meanings.

_____ 8. Adobe   A. an area surrounded by rooms of an Aztec home

_____ 9. Cacao bean   B. Spanish name for a corn pancake

_____ 10. Chicle   C. a type of brick

_____ 11. Corn   D. an Aztec school

_____ 12. Jade   E. maize

_____ 13. Patio   F. Huetzin's father carved this to make decorations

_____ 14. Tortilla   G. an ingredient of chewing gum comes from this tree

_____ 15. Telpuchalli   H. this is used to make chocolate

Name _____ Date _____

AZTEC DAILY LIFE—WORD SCRAMBLE

Unscramble the following groups of letters to form words that were used in the chapter on Aztec daily life.

1. boaed _____

2. atopi _____

3. famnsratc _____

4. gavewin _____

5. thincolol _____

6. zaemi _____

7. licih pesprep _____

8. lartloit _____

9. lechic _____

10. lotochace _____

11. ccCmaela _____

12. gameyu _____

13. aedj _____

14. mtaes _____

15. pchllielTua _____

AZTEC SOCIETY

The clan was the basis of all Aztec society and government. Each person was a member of an extended family. The extended family included grandparents, aunts, and uncles, as well as parents, brothers, and sisters. Groups of the extended families joined to form clans. Twenty clans combined to form a tribe.

Calpolli was the Aztec word for a clan. Calpolli came from the Aztec word calli, which meant "house." Although some nobles owned their own land, the calpolli owned most of the land. The clan divided its land among the families.

At age 13, Aztec children began attending the Telpuchcalli, a school operated by the clan.

Each calpolli elected its own officers to run its business. The calpolli was a true democracy. Most of the important decisions were made by popular vote. Aztec women did not have the right to vote, however.

Aztec tribes met together often to take care of common needs. Each tribe chose a leader to be in the council. The members of the council then chose one of the leaders to be its chief. The chief was in charge of civil and religious affairs. The council enforced the laws of the clan. They also punished wrong doers. The council elected a second chief to be in charge of war matters.

The calpolli expected all of its able-bodied men to fight in any wars. The men considered it an honor in addition to a duty to fight for their clan.

All aspects of its members' lives were governed by the calpolli. At the birth of a child, the parents consulted the calpolli's priest. The priest looked in the book of fate to see if the birth date was lucky. Four days later, the family held a feast to celebrate the birth and give the child a name. During the celebrations, family members showed weapons and tools to baby boys. They showed weaving items and musical instruments to the baby girls.

The Aztecs taught the children in their homes. They taught the boys methods of hunting and fishing or crafts. The women taught the girls spinning, weaving, cooking, and other household duties. At about age 13, the children went to schools operated by their clans. There, the boys learned about weapons and methods of war and the girls learned additional homemaking skills as well as music and dance.

The family arranged for all marriages. The boy and girl involved usually gave their consent to be married. A young person could only marry someone outside the clan. During the wedding ceremonies, the priest tied the cloaks of the bride and groom together. This was a symbol of the joining together of the two. The bride then became a member of her husband's clan.

Name _____ Date _____

QUESTIONS FOR CONSIDERATION

1. What was the clan the basis of?

_____

2. What did 20 clans form?

_____

3. What was the Aztec word for clan?

_____

4. What did each Aztec tribe choose a leader to be in?

_____

5. What was the chief in charge of?

_____

_____

6. What was a second chief chosen to be in charge of?

_____

_____

7. What was the council in charge of?

_____

_____

8. What type of book did the priest look in when a baby was born? Why?

_____

_____

9. How old were Aztec children when they began school?

_____

10. During the wedding ceremonies, what did the priest tie together?

_____

_____

Name _____ Date _____

AZTEC SOCIETY—CROSSWORD

Use the clues below to complete the crossword puzzle.

ACROSS

2. An Aztec baby girl was shown _____ instruments soon after her birth.
4. These were tied together in the Aztec wedding ceremony.
5. Baby Aztec boys were shown these soon after their birth.
8. This person looked in the book of fate to see if a birth was on a lucky day.
9. Twenty family groups (see #1) joined together to form one of these.
10. Aztec women did not have the right to _____ .
12. Title of the man in charge of civil and religious affairs.
13. A _____ became a member of her husband's clan.

DOWN

1. Groups of Aztec families joined to form one of these.
3. Leaders from each Aztec group formed this organization to run its business.
4. The name of the Aztec government unit. It came from the Aztec word for house.
6. Each Aztec was a member of an _____ family.
7. A government run by the people.
9. Children went to school at this age.
11. All able-bodied men had to _____ .

AZTEC RELIGION

Xochitl had a difficult time falling asleep. The excitement of tomorrow's festival kept her mind occupied until she finally became drowsy. Tomorrow, she would attend Ochpaniztli, the festival of the eleventh month. This celebration honored Tlazolteotl, the earth mother goddess. Each month of the calendar had a festival with music, dancing, processions, and sacrifices.

The Aztecs worshipped many gods and goddesses. Each village and each occupation had its own patron god. A different god also watched over each day and each division of the day. The people worshipped the various gods and goddesses to attract the good forces of nature and to repel harmful powers.

Just before the Sun rose, distant sounds of the temple drums woke Xochitl. She dressed quickly, and as she went into the main room of the house, she saw that the rest of the family was already awake and making preparations to go to the temple for the festival

Huitzilopochtli was the Aztec Sun god and god of war. He was also the chief god of Tenochtitlan.

of Ochpaniztli. Her mother gave her a basket of corn to place on the temple altar as a tribute to the goddess Tlazolteotl.

Xochitl was glad that her family arrived as soon as they did. Even though it was still early, hundreds of people had arrived and were lining the road leading to the temple. Xochitl's family was still able to find a location that would give them a good view of the procession.

The crowd quieted down as the beat of the drums stopped. Though they were too far away from the temple to hear what was said, Xochitl knew that the priests were now presenting the sacred chants. The chants provided magic to avoid rains at harvest and to celebrate the refreshment of Earth Mother Tlazolteotl. Xochitl knew that the next part of the ceremony would be a human sacrifice to appease the gods.

In this ceremony, a young woman impersonating the goddess of ripe corn would be the sacrifice. This was one of the few Aztec ceremonies that sacrificed a young woman. Usually the victims of the sacrifices were men who were either captives of wars or slaves. Many of the Aztec religious festivals included human sacrifices. The priest cut open the victim's chest and tore out the heart. He then placed the victim's heart on the altar of the god or goddess. In one ceremony to the god Tlaloc, sacrifices even included children. Xochitl's mother had explained the Aztec belief that the blood given in sacrifice gave the gods new strength and energy.

When Xochitl heard the drums and other music begin, she knew it was time for the grand procession. First came the young men of each clan, dressed in their finest ceremonial outfits. Xochitl enjoyed the colorful display of brightly painted clothing and fancy feather work that decorated the clothes. Each clan member also carried a military weapon and shield decorated with the insignia of the clan.

86

Xochitl watched closely until she recognized her clan's group. Pride filled Xochitl's heart as they passed. She especially enjoyed seeing her uncles and cousins in the procession. She knew that when he was older, her brother would also march with them.

After the last clan passed, groups of warriors with special rank and privileges passed by. Two of the special groups, The Knights of the Eagle and the Knights of the Jaguar, wore animal skins to represent their mascot. These two groups then staged a mock battle to entertain the crowd.

The rest of the festival day was spent visiting friends and feasting. Occasionally other special events provided entertainment and excitement. Other contests and games filled the afternoon. The most important of the games was tlachti. This was a fast-moving game using a rubber ball. Each team tried to score points by putting the ball through rings on the sides of the playing field.

The festival was over by sunset. Xochitl and her family returned home. After the evening meal, Xochitl went to bed early. She had had a busy and tiring day, but in 20 days she would be ready to celebrate the next festival.

AZTEC GODS AND GODDESSES

The ancient Aztecs worshipped over 60 gods and goddesses. This is a list of the more important ones.

NAME	DESCRIPTION
TEZCATLIPOCA	Sun god, most powerful of all gods, chief god of the town of Texcoco
HUITZILOPOCHTLI	Sun god and god of war, chief god of the town of Tenochtitlan
TLAZOLTEOTL	Mother of gods, earth goddess
TLALOC	Rain god, most important to the farmers
QUETZALCOATL	God of learning and the priesthood, also god of arts and crafts
CHICOMECOATL	Goddess of crops
CENETEOTL	God of corn
XIPE TOTEC	God of spring, planting, and re-growth
TONATIUH	A Sun god
MICTLANTECUHLI	God of the dead
XIUHTECUHTLI	Ancient fire god
CHALCHIHUITLICUE	Our Lady of the Turquoise skirt, lakes and rivers

Name _____ Date _____

QUESTIONS FOR CONSIDERATION

1. What was the Aztec name for the festival of the eleventh month?

_____

2. Who was Tlazolteotl?

_____

_____

3. What did each Aztec occupation have?

_____

4. In the story, what was Xochitl going to place on the temple altar?

_____

5. What did the priest present during religious ceremonies?

_____

_____

6. What did many Aztec festivals include?

_____

7. What did the grand procession begin with?

_____

_____

8. What were the names of the two Aztec warrior groups?

_____

_____

9. How were the warrior groups distinguished from other groups?

_____

_____

10. What game that the Aztecs played on their festival days might be similar to a game people play today?

_____

Name _____ Date _____

AZTEC RELIGION WORD SEARCH

Find and circle the following words in the puzzle. The words may be placed horizontally, vertically, or diagonally. They may be spelled forward or backward.

WORD LIST

CENETEOTL	MICTLANTECUHLI	TLAZOLTEOTL
CHALCHIHUITLICUE	QUETZALCOATL	TONATIUH
CHICOMECOATL	TEZCATLIPOCA	XIPE TOTEC
HUITZILOPOCHTLI	TLALOC	XIUHTECUHTLI
FESTIVAL	CHANTS	HUMAN SACRIFICE
PATRON GOD	TEMPLE	PROCESSION
TLACHTI	INSIGNIA	

```
H  T  O  K  W  E  M  I  C  T  L  A  N  T  E  C  U  H  L  I
W  Y  H  I  N  C  H  Z  E  L  P  Z  A  T  V  A  T  Q  D  U
M  S  N  C  K  H  C  K  P  R  O  C  E  S  S  I  O  N  Q  R
X  U  U  C  Z  R  E  C  I  F  I  R  C  A  S  N  A  M  U  H
X  G  N  H  S  D  O  G  N  O  R  T  A  P  X  D  V  N  V  H
K  S  L  A  B  Z  W  V  G  L  A  P  C  F  Q  C  K  R  S  K
R  N  L  L  J  O  G  H  U  I  T  A  N  O  T  F  H  E  I  T
Y  K  B  C  P  W  L  G  Y  T  Q  C  E  T  O  T  E  P  I  X
T  T  I  H  G  L  T  O  E  T  E  N  E  C  N  N  H  G  B  O
E  L  N  I  U  F  C  H  A  N  T  S  Q  K  R  C  C  G  P  E
Z  A  S  H  M  Z  I  A  I  L  T  H  U  C  E  T  H  U  I  X
C  Z  I  U  H  U  I  T  Z  I  L  O  P  O  C  H  T  L  I  B
A  O  G  I  C  P  X  L  U  X  J  I  M  X  T  E  M  P  L  E
T  L  N  T  R  T  Q  B  A  N  T  L  A  L  O  C  K  Y  S  D
L  T  I  L  H  L  H  O  V  V  L  F  E  Z  A  Q  T  Q  T  I
I  E  A  I  Y  A  D  H  C  H  I  C  O  M  E  C  O  A  T  L
P  O  Y  C  S  C  C  V  Z  T  G  T  P  T  D  J  A  N  J  I
O  T  L  U  R  H  G  A  D  Z  C  F  S  J  A  V  Q  F  J  X
C  L  V  E  L  T  A  O  C  L  A  Z  T  E  U  Q  V  X  L  X
A  Z  B  L  B  I  U  I  P  A  N  H  M  W  F  C  Y  C  J  X
```

THE AZTEC CALENDAR

The Aztecs, like the Mayas and ancient Egyptians, used two different calendars. The first calendar was similar to the one created by the Mayas and handed down through the ages. It was a lunar calendar based on the phases of the Moon. The lunar calendar had 260 days. The Aztecs divided their calendar into 13 months, each having 20 days. They thought this calendar was magical. The priests used the lunar calendar to decide which days would be used for religious ceremonies and rituals. Priests also used this calendar to decide which days were lucky and should be used for important activities such as planting crops or going into battle.

The image of the Sun god Tonatiuh is carved in the center of the Aztec calendar stone. Others carvings represent the Aztec days and religious symbols.

A number of dots represented the months, and each of the 20 days had a name. Each of the days also had a hieroglyph (picture word). The days' names and their hieroglyphs are shown below:

| Cipactli **Crocodile** | Ehecatl **Wind** | Calli **House** | Cuetzpallin **Lizard** | Coatl **Serpent** |
| Miquiztli **Death's-head** | Mazatl **Deer** | Tochtli **Rabbit** | Atl **Water** | Itzcuintli **Dog** |

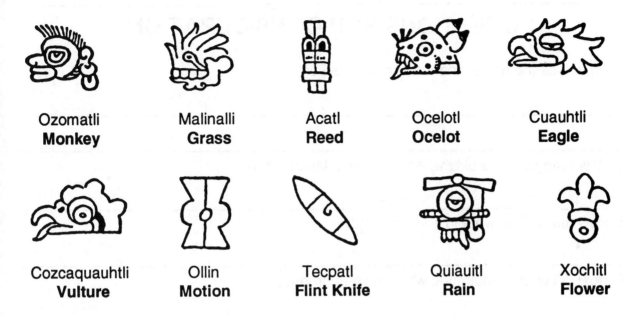

| Ozomatli **Monkey** | Malinalli **Grass** | Acatl **Reed** | Ocelotl **Ocelot** | Cuauhtli **Eagle** |

| Cozcaquauhtli **Vulture** | Ollin **Motion** | Tecpatl **Flint Knife** | Quiauitl **Rain** | Xochitl **Flower** |

Our New Year's day would have appeared on the Aztec calendar as:

(one dot = first month   crocodile = first day)

The Aztecs established their second calendar on the movement of the Sun. Similar to our calendar today, it had 365 days based on the time it took the earth to orbit the Sun. They divided their solar calendar into 18 months each containing 20 days. The extra five days were "nothing" days added to the end of each year. The Aztecs thought these five days were unlucky, so they did not give them names. The Aztec stopped all activities during the five "nothing" days. At the end of the five days, they gave a sacrificial victim in tribute to the gods.

Our calendar has centuries using 100-year divisions. Both of the Aztec calendars used 52-year divisions. The Aztecs had a major celebration at the start of each new 52-year cycle. Part of the celebration included the New Fire Ceremony. The priests extinguished the temple's altar fires, and the citizens let their household fires go out. At midnight of the new era, the priest would light a fire on the chest of a sacrificial victim. The people would then light a fire stick from the altar fire and use it to light their home fires.

One of the important artifacts from the Aztecs is the famous calendar stone. Discovered in 1790, the stone is about 12 feet in diameter and weights 20 tons. In the center of the stone is an image of the Sun god Tonatiuh. Other carvings on the stone represent the Aztec days and religious symbols. Aztec priests may have placed the hearts of sacrificial victims on the stone's center during religious ceremonies.

Name _____ Date _____

QUESTIONS FOR CONSIDERATION

1. What was the Aztec lunar calendar based on?

_____

_____

2. How many months did the Aztec lunar calendar have?

_____

3. How many days were in a lunar month?

_____

4. How did priests determine when to plant crops?

_____

_____

5. What was the second Aztec calendar based on?

_____

_____

6. How many days did this calendar have?

_____

7. How many months did this calendar have?

_____

8. How many days were in a month?

_____

9. How did Aztecs deal with the fact that there were five extra days in the second calendar?

_____

_____

10. What was discovered in 1790?

_____

_____

Name _____ Date _____

AZTEC CALENDAR ACTIVITY

Create a make-believe Aztec calendar for this month. For each day, include the hieroglyph, the Aztec name, and the English definition. Use the examples given in this chapter. You will have to repeat the names and hieroglyphs or make up some of your own. Perhaps you could make a bulletin board display of your calendar.

THE CITY OF TENOCHTITLAN

The greatest city of the Aztecs was Tenochtitlan. The early settlers built the village on an island in Lake Texcoco. They chose the island since the lake protected them against attacks from the mainland.

A twin village, Tlaltelolco, was on another island to the north. The natives soon built a bridge between the two villages, but the two villages then became rivals.

The great pyramid and double temple to the gods Huitzilopochtli and Tlaloc was the most impressive structure in the plaza of Tenochtitlan.

After a short battle, Tenochtitlan defeated and absorbed Tlaltelolco.

As the villages grew into a city, the people needed more land. They dug mud from the lake bottom and piled it into mounds. The city became criss-crossed by canals. Tenochtitlan reminded the Europeans of Venice. The canals became the major streets of the city. Soon three large earthen causeways linked the city to the mainland. These causeways became the major entrances into the city. The three causeways joined at the great plaza in the center of the city.

Tenochtitlan had four major units. These units had a total of 20 sections. Each clan had its own section of the city that contained the houses and gardens of the clan members. Each clan also had its own temple and school.

The great plaza was in the center of the city. It measured 520 by 600 feet and had over 60 buildings. The most impressive structure in the plaza was the pyramid and double temple to the gods Huitzilopochtli and Tlaloc. It was over 200 feet tall.

Four other temples and the sacred ball court were built in the great plaza. Other buildings in the plaza included the home of the priest, the house of a military unit, and the great palace of the ruler Montezuma. A large market place and the now-famous calendar stone were also in the great plaza.

The Spanish first arrived in Tenochtitlan in November 1519. Hernando Cortés led the Spanish invaders. Tenochtitlan amazed them when they entered. One of the men wrote that he thought what he saw was a dream. The population of the city when the Spanish arrived is estimated at between 200,000 and 300,000 people. It was larger than any city in Europe at the time.

Cortes and his men soon defeated the Aztecs, and Tenochtitlan became a Spanish city. It continued to change after the Spanish conquest. In the 1600s the Spanish drained the lake. Today Mexico's capital, Mexico City, lies on the ruins of Tenochtitlan. The Mexican president's palace is on the location that was once Montezuma's palace.

Name _____ Date _____

QUESTIONS FOR CONSIDERATION

1. Where was the village that later became Tenochtitlan built?

_____

2. What could be found on an island nearby?

_____

3. What became Tenochtitlan's major streets?

_____

4. What linked the city to the mainland?

_____

5. What did each clan have?

_____

_____

6. What was in the center of the city?

_____

_____

7. How tall was the great temple?

_____

8. What did one of the Spanish conquerors think the city he saw was?

_____

_____

9. How big was Tenochtitlan when the Spanish arrived? How many cities of similar size might they have seen in Europe?

_____

_____

10. What now stands where Tenochtitlan once did?

_____

Name _____ Date _____

THE CITY OF TENOCHTITLAN—CROSSWORD

Use the clues below to complete the crossword puzzle.

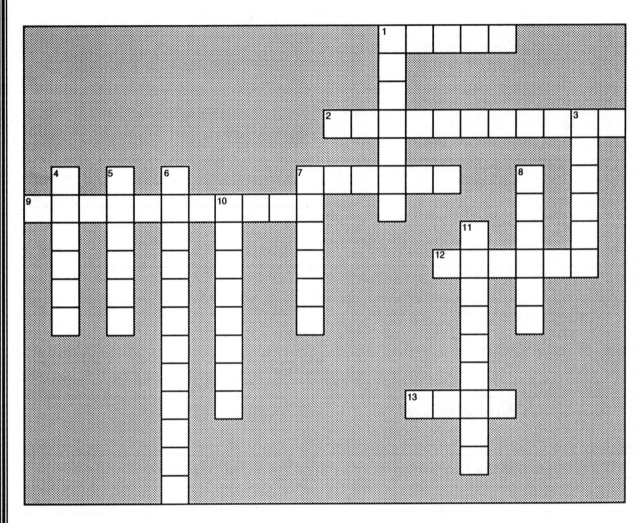

ACROSS

1. This was in the center of the city.
2. Tenochtitlan's twin village.
7. The capital of this country was built on the ancient city's ruins.
9. Tenochtitlan was built on an island in _____ _____ .
12. These waterways were the main streets of the city.
13. Each _____ had its own section of the city.

DOWN

1. Shape of the most impressive structure in the city.
3. This Spanish leader conquered the Aztecs.
4. This trading place was also in the center of the city.
5. The greatest structure in the city was this double worship place.
6. This was the Aztecs' greatest city.
7. The Aztecs created more land by making these out of mud from the bottom of the lake.
8. This was the home of the ruler, Montezuma.
10. This famous stone was in the center of the city.
11. These raised structures linked the city to the mainland.

AZTEC ART

Two serpents form her head. She has claws instead of hands and feet. Her skirt consists of many twisting snakes, and she wears a necklace made of human hearts and hands. Coatlicue, the goddess of the earth, stands nine and one-half feet tall. This shocking sight is one of the most famous Aztec sculptures.

The best remaining examples of Aztec art are its architecture and sculpture. Aztec sculpture remains among the most elaborate in the Americas. Almost all Aztec art used religious subjects and themes.

The temple was the most magnificent structure in each Aztec town. It was visible from miles away and stood on the top of huge pyramid structures. Great staircases rose up the sides of the pyramid. The great pyramid at Tenochtitlan had two temples at its peak.

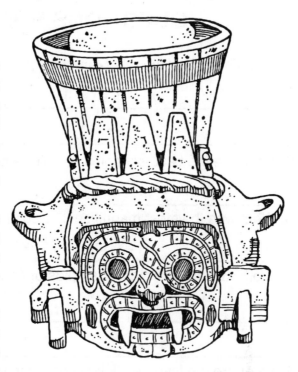

This ceramic vessel is adorned with the image of Tlaloc, the god of rain.

Most of the sculpture came from decorations of the temple. The sculpture used a variety of subjects. Animals and representations of the gods were favorite subjects. We still can see examples of sculptures of spiders. Some of the sculpture is huge, like the calendar stone weighing over 20 tons, and some is very small and delicate.

The Aztecs used a variety of material for their sculpture. Stone was the most often used material. However, examples of Aztec art remain that were made of wood, jade, turquoise, emerald, and volcanic glass.

The Aztecs also made items of metal. They used metals easily found in nature. They did not know how to use iron or how to mix metals for great strength. Aztec workers used stone instead of metal tools. The craftsmen shaped gold, copper, and some silver into beautiful jewelry and decorations. Most of the Aztec gold treasures no longer exist. After conquering the Aztecs, Cortés and the Spaniards took the gold art works to Europe. The king of Spain had the treasures melted down to reuse the gold.

Aztec craftsmen also made clay pottery. Some of it was plain and for everyday use. The Aztec kitchens contained many clay jars and other utensils. They also created elaborate and brightly colored ritual pottery.

Aztec women spent much of their time weaving cloth. They dyed, embroidered, and decorated the cloth. The higher a person's social status, the more elaborate the decorations that appeared on his clothing. The Aztecs also excelled at feather weaving. Weavers raised exotic birds in cages to get brightly colored feathers. The weavers attached the feathers to a net to make cloaks, headdresses, and other decorative items. Only one example of Aztec feather weaving survives today. A headdress given by Montezuma to Cortés is preserved in a museum in Vienna.

Name _____ Date _____

QUESTIONS FOR CONSIDERATION

1. Describe one of the most famous Aztec sculptures.

_____

_____

2. What are the best examples of Aztec art in existence today?

_____

3. What was the most magnificent structure in each Aztec town?

_____

4. From where have most examples of Aztec sculpture come?

_____

_____

5. What are the favorite subjects of Aztec sculpture?

_____

_____

6. What was the material used most often by the Aztecs for their sculpture?

_____

7. What is one of the largest Aztec sculptures? How much does it weigh?

_____

8. What did the Spanish do with many of the Aztec works of art?

_____

_____

9. How did Aztecs get the feathers to make headresses and cloaks?

_____

10. What, if any, examples of Aztec feather weaving are still in existence today?

_____

_____

Name _____ Date _____

AZTEC ART—WORD SCRAMBLE

Unscramble the letters of the words listed below to make words that were used in the article on Aztec Arts and Crafts. (Hint: capital letters can help you find the word)

1. terspnse _____

2. luicCteoa _____

3. latnetoTcinh _____

4. tusrepclu _____

5. ueiqsrtou _____

6. daje _____

7. werejly _____

8. ylac toerpty _____

9. taerfeh givwaen _____

10. ddeessrah _____

11. oenMzaumt _____

12. draanlec _____

13. eelmard _____

14. soCret _____

15. prdeiss _____

AZTEC GAMES

Tlachtli was an Aztec game played on a court. It seems to have been similar to a combination of modern basketball and soccer.

Tlachtli became the most important Aztec game. Tlachtli was a ball game similar to a Mayan game named pok-a-tok. Tlachtli began as a sport and later became a ritual game. The Aztecs played it during religious ceremonies. They played the game as entertainment for the ruler and priests as well as for the common people. Sometimes, the Aztecs sacrificed the losers to the gods.

We do not know the rules of the Mayan game, but all large Mayan and Aztec cities had game courts. The Mayan city, Chichén Itzá, had seven game courts. The largest court was 545 feet long and 225 feet wide. A basket was at each end of the court. The Mayas decorated the basket as a snake. It was 35 feet high.

The Aztec courts were similar to the Mayan courts. They were often near the temple areas. The courts were in the shape of a capital "I". They had seats on both sides for viewers. A vertical stone ring was in the middle of the side walls. The object of the game was to put the ball through the ring. A team also scored a point if the other team let the ball touch the ground.

Tlachtli used a hard, rubber ball about six inches in diameter. The players wore padding. They could not touch the ball with their hands. The ball could only be moved by the players' hips, knees, legs, and elbows.

The Aztecs also played board games. The most popular was *patolli*. It was similar to parcheesi or backgammon. However, we do not know the exact rules of patolli. The Aztecs played it on a cross-shaped design painted on a board or mat. They used beans painted with dots as dice. They used beans or kernels of maize as markers. The object of the game was to move around the board and return to home base. The Aztec often played patolli as a gambling game. The Aztec ruler Montezuma and the Spanish conqueror Cortés may have played patolli while Montezuma was a captive.

Name _____ Date _____

QUESTIONS FOR CONSIDERATION

1. What was the most important game of the Aztecs?

_____

2. To what game was it similar?

_____

3. How many game courts did Chichén Itzá have?

_____

4. How did the Mayas decorate the basket?

_____

_____

5. What was the shape of the game courts?

_____

6. What was the object of the game?

_____

_____

7. Of what substance was the ball made?

_____

8. In what way could players not touch the ball?

_____

_____

9. What was the name of the popular Aztec board game?

_____

10. What did the Aztecs use as dice?

_____

_____

Name _____ Date _____

AZTEC GAMES

On this page is a drawing of the ancient Aztec board game patolli. You could make a larger drawing of the board on another piece of paper. The Aztecs used beans marked with dots as dice. They used beans or kernels of maize as markers.

We do not know the rules of the Aztec game. Make up your own game rules. Perhaps, you could have a patolli tournament.

AZTEC AGRICULTURE

Aztec methods of farming were similar to those of the Mayan and Incan tribes. The Aztecs used a pointed stick to plant the crops. One person would make a hole in the ground with the stick. Another person would put the seeds in the hole and then cover the seeds with soil. The Aztecs never invented a plow to turn the earth.

The Aztecs created more farmland by forming small islands called chinampas in swamps and lakes.

The slash and burn method of agriculture was used by the Aztecs. They chopped down forest areas and left the trees and brush to dry in the heat of the Sun for many days. The farmers then burned the areas to clear them. The ashes of the burnt trees provided fertilizer. The farmers then planted the new crops in the clearings.

Chinampas were the most interesting development of Aztec agriculture. Chinampas were small islands formed in lake and swamp areas. The farmers made them by digging the mud at the bottom of the lake or swamp and piling it into little mounds or islands. The Aztecs then planted crops and gardens on the chinampas. They are sometimes called floating gardens even though they did not really float.

The Aztec farmers also cut terraces into hillsides to create more farm land. They made many canals to help carry water to the fields.

Corn, called maize by the Indians, was the main crop. The Aztec farmers also grew avocados, as well as many varieties of beans, squash, sweet potatoes, and tomatoes. Different crops came from the lowlands. Major lowland crops included cotton, papayas, rubber, and cacao beans, from which chocolate is made.

After the harvest, farmers brought the crops to the marketplace in the nearest city. The Aztecs did not use animals or wheeled vehicles to move crops. The men carried everything to the market on their backs. In some of the distant villages, farmers used dugout canoes to move crops over rivers and canals.

The market was in the center of each town. Some of the markets were very large. The market in the city of Tlatelolco was the largest. The Spaniard Hernando Cortés wrote that over 60,000 persons visited the market each day.

The Aztecs, like other Indian tribes, did not use money. They used a barter system. Barter is trading objects rather than buying and selling them. The markets contained many other things for barter. Other items traded included weapons, animals, household goods, rare colorful feathers, and even slaves.

Name _____ Date _____

QUESTIONS FOR CONSIDERATION

1. What tool did the Aztecs never use in agriculture? What did they use instead?

_____

2. What provided fertilizer to crop grounds?

_____

3. What were chinampas?

_____

_____

4. What are chinampas sometimes called?

_____

5. What was the main crop of the Aztecs?

_____

6. From what is chocolate made?

_____

7. How did farmers carry all of their goods to the market?

_____

_____

8. What would farmers from distant villages use to bring goods to the market?

_____

_____

9. Who wrote about visiting an Aztec market?

_____

10. What is trading, rather than buying and selling objects, known as?

_____

_____

Name _____ Date _____

AZTEC AGRICULTURE—WORD SCRAMBLE

Unscramble the following groups of letters to form words that were used in the chapter on Aztec Agriculture.

1. aocac nesba _____

2. otcotn _____

3. temasoot _____

4. imaez _____

5. saaappy _____

6. saneb _____

7. haquesss _____

8. weste tootsape _____

9. rerbub _____

10. vasodaco _____

11. naichmasp _____

12. zleiifetrr _____

13. serercat _____

14. llaocTloet _____

15. rearbt _____

AZTEC MEDICINE

Ancient Aztec medicine was a combination of religion, belief in magical powers, and the use of plants and herbs to make medicine. The Aztecs believed that illness had one of three causes. They believed that some illnesses were punishments sent from an angry god or goddess. They also thought that an enemy could use

Aztec doctors made medicines out of plants, roots, herbs, and barks.

black magic to cause an illness. The third source of an illness might be from natural causes.

Aztecs practiced magic to avoid illnesses. They often wore amulets as protection. An amulet is a good luck charm. It is a small ornament worn to keep away harm and evil.

The priests often tended the sick. If the illness was serious, the *ticitl* was called in. The ticitl was a "cure doctor" or a "shaman." The ticitl rubbed the body of the patient to remove the "magic dart." The magic dart was an object that they believed entered the body and caused the illness.

Aztec doctors also used plants, roots, herbs, and barks to make medicines. Most of the plants and herbs used were sacred to the rain god Tlaloc. The two plants used most often were *yauhtli* and *iztauhyatl*. They used both plants to cure fevers, epilepsy, stiffness, swelling, colds, and coughs. The Aztecs also believed the plants had magical powers to cure love sickness.

The doctors used the plants and herbs in many ways. They often rubbed parts of the plants on the skin to relieve aches and pains. Sometimes the doctor had patients inhale the fragrance of a plant or smoke from the burning plant. Often the doctors ground dried plants or combined them with liquids into medicines. Another favorite source of medicine was the sap from the maguey plant. They used the sap in the treatment of battle wounds and other injuries.

Ticitl were also skilled surgeons. They used knives made of volcanic glass to perform surgery. After doctors cut out a tumor, they covered the wound with crushed plants to speed its healing.

The Spanish invaders studied Indian medicine. Between 1547 and 1585, Bernardino de Sahagún wrote about Aztec medicine. Indian doctors treated Hernando Cortés' wounds after a battle. Cortés later wrote to King Charles V of Spain that the Indian doctors were just as good as the Spanish doctors.

Name _____ Date _____

QUESTIONS FOR CONSIDERATION

1. What was ancient Aztec medicine a combination of?

_____

_____

2. What types of things did Aztecs believe caused sickness?

_____

_____

3. Why did Aztecs wear amulets?

_____

_____

4. What was a ticitl?

_____

_____

5. Why did Aztec doctors rub patients' bodies?

_____

_____

6. What did Aztec doctors use to make medicines?

_____

_____

7. What were the most common medicines?

_____

8. What did Aztec doctors use to heal battle wounds?

_____

9. What were Aztec surgeons' knives made of?

_____

10. How good were Aztec doctors?

_____

Name _____ Date _____

AZTEC MEDICINE—WORD SEARCH

Find and circle the following words in the puzzle. The words may be placed horizontally, vertically, or diagonally. They may be spelled forward or backward.

WORD LIST

AMULET	MAGIC	ROOTS	BARKS
MAGUEY	SHAMAN	HERBS	NATURAL CAUSES
SURGEONS	PLANTS	CURE DOCTOR	MEDICINES
WOUNDS	TLALOC	YAUHTLI	TICITL
KNIVES	FEVERS	IZTAUHYATL	MAGIC DART

```
S Q V M K L I S G M A G U E Y U G H B U
U Y B A W T A Y E I Z T A U H Y A T L O
R A W O Y D J Q N S R J N A M A H S X S
G U E V T L L U M Y U Q P L A N T S N H
E H F M J T T Q Z G T A V T C E Z S P I
O T M S O R S I Y K U L C O C Y D Y C B
N L S D L N P D C V Y O A L K L H F M V
S I I T C N R K N I T Y T L A F D Y A H
B P Q W O V T Y A U T B L O O R J P I T
D E N Z X O G K R C O W A Y S C U Q J L
K P G Y V V R M O S O W F W K J U T O O
D S R E V E F X T J G C P S E Q P I A D
H Q Z H E R B S C L P I N K X A B T E N
N W P B A R K S O D W G P O E J M E O Z
L E Z A E R M I D D C A M V O C X D J R
G I S I A S K Q E L K M O T E L U M A Z
Y M U L I E A T R R R J U G O F D E S J
P C P O R R M T U Y I S E V I N K M K K
M D A L P D Z X C G A M E D I C I N E S
Q S A T W Q T A P H T R A D C I G A M K
```

AZTEC WARFARE

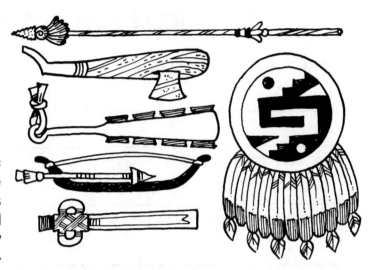

Warfare was an important part of Aztec life. Every able-bodied Aztec man participated in fighting. The Aztecs believed it was a religious duty to be a warrior.

At the age of about 13, Aztec boys attended a school named the telpuchalli. At this school, the boys learned how to use weapons and the basics of warfare. Each boy would follow an experienced warrior into battle. It was important for the warrior to take captives. The Aztec honored the men who took many captives. The successful warriors often received social rank, land, or important offices as their reward.

Aztec warriors were armed with slings, javelins, clubs, bows and arrows, and swords called macuahuitls. Warriors also carried shields decorated with paint and feathers.

Aztec warriors used many weapons. The macuahuitl was the most important. It was a sword edged with sharp pieces of obsidian glass. The Aztecs also used bows and arrows, javelins, clubs, and slings.

The warriors carried shields and wore padded cotton armor. They decorated the shield with paint and feathers. They also wore brightly colored feather headdresses. They did not have uniforms. Each warrior dressed as he wished. They often had the sign of their group on their shield. The main warrior groups were the Order of the Eagle, the Order of the Jaguar, and the Order of the Arrows.

Battles did not last long. They did not use animals to carry supplies. The soldiers had to carry all of their supplies, so they did not have enough food and weapons to support a long attack. Most of the fighting was hand-to-hand combat. The first tribe to retreat was the loser.

The Aztecs went to war for two main reasons. They fought to get tribute and the needed supply of sacrificial victims for religious ceremonies.

The tribe that lost the battle had to give the winning tribe gold, jewels, crops, and other valuable items. Tribute was everything the losing tribe had to give to the winning tribe. Often, the losing tribe paid tribute each year for many years after the battle. Tribute from many defeated tribes helped keep the Aztecs strong and powerful.

The goal of Aztec warfare was to capture rather than kill the enemy. Members of the losing tribe became slaves or sacrifices. Aztec religion demanded many human sacrifices to please the gods.

Name _____ Date _____

QUESTIONS FOR CONSIDERATION

1. Why were most Aztec men warriors?

_____

_____

2. Where did Aztec boys learn to fight?

_____

3. How were Aztec boys trained to fight?

_____

_____

4. What were successful warriors given?

_____

5. What was the macuahuitl?

_____

_____

6. Did Aztec warriors wear armor? If so, describe it.

_____

_____

7. Why were Aztec battles often short?

_____

_____

8. How were the winning and losing tribes determined?

_____

9. Why did Aztecs go to war?

_____

_____

10. What was the goal of Aztec warfare?

_____

Name _____ Date _____

AZTEC WARFARE—CROSSWORD

Use the clues below to complete the crossword puzzle.

ACROSS

2. The Aztec warrior did not have this. Each dressed as he wished.
3. Aztec soldiers wore padded armor made of this.
6. This Aztec weapon was a sword edged with sharp pieces of glass.
10. This was decorated with feathers and paint. It often contained the sign of the fighting group.
11. Aztecs believed fighting in a war was this type of duty.
13. Aztec weapons included spears, _____, and slings.
14. Successful warriors might receive social rank, _____, or important offices.

DOWN

1. Losing tribes gave this to the winners.
3. It was more important to the Aztecs to take live _____ rather than kill the enemy.
4. Aztecs fought to get tribute and sacrificial _____.
5. Members of the losing tribe often became these.
7. Aztec warriors wore these made of brightly colored feathers.
8. Most fighting was hand-to-hand _____.
9. One of the Aztec warrior groups was the Order of the _____.
12. Aztec boys learned the skills of warfare at this school.

THE ARRIVAL OF THE SPANIARDS

When Montezuma met Cortés, he though the Spaniard was the god Quetzalcoatl returning from across the sea, so he did not oppose the Spanish.

Soon after Columbus landed in the Americas in 1492, the Spanish began settlements in the "new world." The Spanish governor of Cuba sent expeditions into Mexico in 1517 and 1518. Hernando Cortés headed the third expedition in 1519. They were looking for riches and slave labor for the plantations in Cuba. Cortés and his men, known as Conquistadors, encountered the Aztecs.

Cortés and his men conquered the Aztecs in just three years. Many Indians helped Cortés defeat the Aztecs. The other Indian tribes resented the heavy taxes they were paying the Aztecs.

The great Aztec chief, Montezuma, did not oppose the Spaniards. He remembered an Aztec legend that said that the powerful god Quetzalcoatl had sailed across the sea and would return someday. Montezuma had never seen white men before. The metal armor of the Spanish also impressed him. Montezuma thought Cortés represented the returning god. Since he offered no resistance, the Spanish took Montezuma prisoner.

In 1520, the Aztecs rebelled against the invaders and drove the Spanish from the city. By May 1521, Cortés and his men returned. They began a bloody attack against the Aztecs. Montezuma died from wounds he received in the attack. The next Aztec ruler, Cuauctemoc, surrendered to the Spanish in August 1521.

The Spanish conquerors destroyed the Aztec cities. They made the Aztecs their slaves. The conquistadors took the Aztecs' gold and other treasures and sent them to Spain. Later, Spanish missionaries arrived. They destroyed Aztec temples and wiped out all traces of the Aztec religion. The religion of the white man soon replaced the old Indian beliefs.

The Indians had little chance against the invaders. The Spanish had better weapons and armor than the Indian tribes. The Spanish also brought a new disease called smallpox with them from Europe. The Indians did not have any resistance to this new infection. Thousands of Indians died from the disease. Many Indian warriors also died from the disease.

After defeating the Aztecs, the Spanish invaders fought the Incas and the Mayas. The Spanish defeated the Incas in 1533. The last city of the Mayas fell in March 1697. The Spanish now had full control of the region.

Name _____ Date _____

QUESTIONS FOR CONSIDERATION

1. Who was the leader of the Spanish conquerors?

_____

2. What were Spanish invaders known as?

_____

3. How long did it take the Spanish to conquer the Aztecs?

_____

4. What was the name of the Aztec chief?

_____

5. In what year did the Aztecs surrender to the Spaniards?

_____

6. Why did the Aztecs have no chance against the Spanish conquerors?

_____

_____

7. What did the Spaniards do with the Aztec gold and treasures that they found?

_____

_____

8. What disease helped the Spanish defeat the Aztecs?

_____

9. What was the next Indian civilization conquered by the Spaniards?

_____

10. How many years were there between the defeat of the Aztecs and the Incas? the Aztecs and the Mayas?

_____

_____

Name _____ Date _____

THE ARRIVAL OF THE SPANIARDS—WORD SCRAMBLE

Unscramble the letters of the words listed below to make words that were used in the article on the Arrival of the Spaniards. (Hint: capital letters can help you find the word)

1. wen rodwl _____

2. denoxetipi _____

3. disCquosranto _____

4. zometanMu _____

5. rreesstau _____

6. iiisssaremon _____

7. psolmxal _____

8. raspinSad _____

9. finecinto _____

10. saverind _____

11. alQeoattlzuc _____

12. ielinrog _____

13. sripoenr _____

14. csnaI _____

15. yaasM _____

ANSWER KEYS

THE ARRIVAL OF MAN–QUESTIONS (page 2)
1. the water formed into ice
2. by crossing the Bering Strait
3. hunting and gathering
4. planting and growing food
5. they could remain in one area
6. mud and branches
7. to store grain
8. early to store food, later also to look attractive
9. garbage dumps
10. spearheads, arrowheads, tools, grinding stones, broken pottery

THE OLMECS–QUESTIONS (page 5)
1. 1200 B.C.
2. 700 to 400 B.C.
3. the Aztecs
4. rubber people
5. San Lorenzo and La Venta
6. giant carved stone heads
7. pyramid
8. glass made by volcanoes
9. mirrors
10. used picture writing, had number system, had calendar

THE OLMECS–WORD SCRAMBLE (page 6)
1. Caribbean
2. rubber
3. San Lorenzo
4. La Venta
5. jade
6. hematite
7. jaguar
8. Olmec
9. Aztec
10. Valley of Mexico
11. calendar
12. Central America
13. volcano
14. mirrors
15. mysterious

TEOTIHUACAN–QUESTIONS (page 8)
1. Mexico City
2. The Altiplano Indians
3. covers over eight square miles
4. Avenue of the Dead
5. Pyramid of the Sun
6. a serpent god
7. brightly-colored wall murals
8. Pieces of their special, thin, orange pottery have been found throughout Mexico.
9. It was destroyed or burned.
10. that the gods built it

TEOTIHUACAN–WORD SEARCH (page 9)

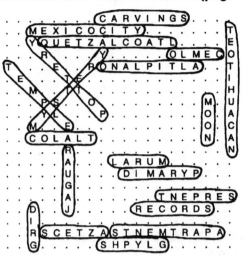

THE MAYAS–QUESTIONS (page 11)
1. rugged highlands and dense swamps
2. short; black hair; painted their bodies blue, black, or red; tattooed; sometimes had crossed eyes and flat foreheads
3. so that their children's eyes might cross
4. to flatten their foreheads
5. fish
6. Pre-Classic Era, 2500 B.C. to A.D. 250; Classic Era, A.D. 250 to 900; Post-Classic, 900 to 1500
7. Tikal
8. advanced systems of mathematics, astronomy, writing
9. what happened to them
10. Christopher Columbus

MAYAN RELIGION–QUESTIONS (page 16)
1. halach uinic
2. a living god
3. high priest
4. ahkin
5. believed it was flat
6. rode on the back of a crocodile
7. corn
8. nine
9. Priests cut out a victim's heart to give to the gods.
10. Victims were asked what messages they brought back from the gods and were given special treatment from then on.

MAYAN RELIGION–MATCHING ACTIVITY (page 17)

1. D
2. G
3. M
4. A
5. H
6. L
7. C
8. F
9. B
10. N
11. E
12. O
13. K
14. J
15. I

MAYAN CITIES–QUESTIONS (page 19)

1. causeways
2. stone
3. Tikal
4. over 100, 000
5. eight
6. Copán
7. five
8. staircase 30 feet wide, with 63 steps. Each step is covered with picture writing.
9. Chichén Itzá
10. observatory

MAYAN CITIES–WORD SCRAMBLE (page 20)

1. Tikal
2. Copan
3. Chichén Itzá
4. pyramids
5. temples
6. plazas
7. peasants
8. causeways
9. Guatemala
10. jaguar
11. jungles
12. limestone
13. sacrifice
14. Double Comb
15. observatory

MAYAN WRITING–QUESTIONS (page 22)

1. the Olmecs
2. glyphs, pictures, or symbols
3. glyphs
4. glued together ficus bark fibers
5. coated it with white lime
6. codex
7. decorated boards
8. they thought they were evil
9. only three complete ones
10. museums in Europe

MAYAN WRITING–WORD SEARCH (page 23)

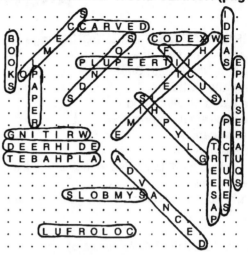

MAYAN MATHEMATICS & ASTRONOMY–QUESTIONS (page 25)

1. zero
2. 20
3. $\overset{\bullet\bullet\bullet}{\rule{2em}{1.5pt}} = 8$ $\overset{\bullet\bullet}{\underset{\rule{2em}{1.5pt}}{\rule{2em}{1.5pt}}} = 12$
4. the movements of the Sun, Moon, planets, and stars
5. It was an observatory
6. sacred calendar: no months, 260 days, 20 day names

secular calendar: 365 days, 18 months of 20 days, five days at end of the year that were part of no month and considered unlucky
7. sacred calendar had no months, 260 rather than 365 days
8. to develop accurate calendars
9. believed they were unlucky
10. the Aztecs

MAYAN MATH EXERCISE (page 26)

0 =
2 = ●●
4 = ●●●●
6 = ●
8 = ●●●
9 = ●●●●
11 = ●

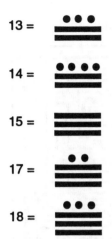

13 =

14 =

15 =

17 =

18 =

Problems at bottom of page

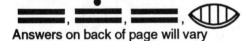

Answers on back of page will vary

MAYAN ARTS AND CRAFTS–QUESTIONS (page 28)
1. cotton
2. black-war; yellow-food; red-blood; blue-sacrifice
3. feather weaving
4. reeds, vines, rushes, and split cane
5. from clay coils smoothed together
6. as tall as a person
7. limestone
8. stela
9. frescoes
10. everyday scenes and religious ceremonies

MAYAN AGRICULTURE–QUESTIONS (page 31)
1. by hunting and gathering
2. too many people to survive just hunting and gathering
3. slash and burn
4. chop trees, let them dry, burn them
5. wore soil out quickly
6. fruit orchards and gardens
7. hemp for rope, cotton for cloth
8. drought
9. put soil in mounds, let water run through ditches formed between mounds
10. He was believed to be the god of rain.

MAYAN AGRICULTURE–WORD SCRAMBLE (page 32)
1. hunters
2. gathers
3. vegetables
4. planting stick
5. orchards
6. maize
7. avocados
8. cacao
9. irrigation
10. terraces
11. swamps
12. chocolate
13. reservoirs
14. hemp
15. mounds

MAYAN TRADE–QUESTIONS (page 34)
1. Ppolm
2. Ek Chaub
3. to Belize and Guatemala
4. to the Caribbean Islands
5. slaves
6. no roads, but many criss-crossing, small pathways
7. 50 feet long, eight feet wide, with cabin and crew
8. Chichén Itzá, Court of a Thousand Columns
9. traded, barter system
10. cacao beans

MAYAN TRADE–WORD SEARCH (PAGE 35)

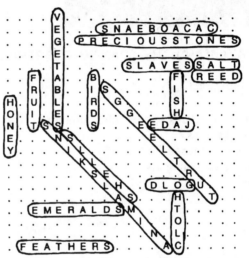

THE GREAT MAYAN MYSTERY–QUESTIONS (page 37)
1. 850 B.C.
2. countryside
3. earthquake, hurricane, disease epidemic
4. the soil was depleted; wouldn't feed the population
5. the use of the plow
6. manpower (foot)
7. peasants
8. peasants provided all the food and wealth for the nobles
9. Toltecs
10. answers will vary

THE GREAT MAYAN MYSTERY–CROSSWORD (page 38)

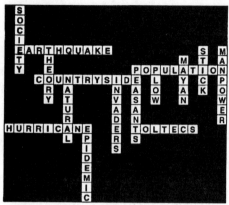

THE MAYAS AND THE SPANISH–QUESTIONS (page 40)

1. Mayapan
2. 1441
3. civil wars, epidemics, droughts, hurricanes
4. gold and slaves
5. smallpox, diseases
6. hundreds of thousands
7. Cortés
8. Mérida
9. 1697
10. Tayasal

THE MAYAS AND THE SPANISH–WORD SCRAMBLE (page 41)

1. Mayapan
2. epidemics
3. Columbus
4. canoes
5. smallpox
6. Hernando Cortes
7. Mérida
8. conquest
9. cavalry
10. Tayasal
11. Spanish
12. slaves
13. disease
14. expeditions
15. Yucatan

THE TOLTECS–QUESTIONS (page 43)

1. A.D. 900–1200
2. Mixcoatl
3. Topiltzin
4. Tula
5. answers will vary, should include warrior
6. human sacrifice
7. temple of Quetzalcoatl
8. A.D. 1150
9. Aztecs
10. yes; Aztecs and many others

THE TOLTECS–MAZE (page 44)

THE INCAS–QUESTIONS (page 46)

1. no system of writing
2. Manco Capac
3. Cuzco
4. Andes Mountains
5. Pachacutec
6. build roads
7. terraces
8. provided transportation, food, and clothing
9. quipus
10. Pizarro

INCAN RELIGION–QUESTIONS (page 49)

1. Virococha
2. Inti
3. gold
4. the study of objects and animals to find hidden meanings and magic signs
5. sacred place or thing
6. 12
7. religious festivals, ceremonies or rituals
8. Capac Raimi, December
9. outside so everyone could come
10 llamas, guinea pigs, humans

INCAN AGRICULTURE–QUESTIONS (page 52)
1. potato
2. 40
3. It would resist the frosts of the region.
4. sara
5. chuñu
6. cut terraces into the mountains
7. dug canals and tunnels, built raised aqueducts
8. irrigation system and terraces still used today
9. answers will vary—crops provided them with the necessary food, yet natural forces influenced crop production greatly
10. after planting season

INCAN AGRICULTURE–WORD SEARCH (page 53)

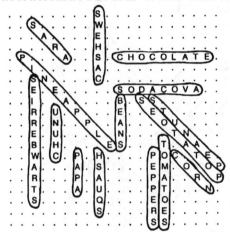

INCAN WEAVING–QUESTIONS (page 55)
1. llama, alpaca, vicuña
2. llama hair
3. clothing
4. silk
5. cotton
6. backstrap
7. copper and tin
8. bright blue
9. shellfish
10. wove garments for the ruler

INCAN WEAVING–CROSSWORD (page 56)

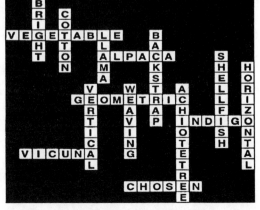

INCAN ARTS AND CRAFTS–QUESTIONS (page 58)
1. bronze
2. work tax
3. gold
4. it was the metal of the Moon
5. melted it down and shipped it to Spain
6. to tie ropes to carry it
7. a jar with a pointed bottom that stood upright when full and laid on its side when empty
8. The method has been lost.
9. black, red, white, yellow, orange
10. yes; pottery, weaving, metal work

INCAN ARTS AND CRAFTS–WORD SCRAMBLE (page 59)
1. weaving
2. metalwork
3. bronze
4. statues
5. silver
6. pottery
7. aryballuses
8. geometric
9. orange
10. designs
11. jewelry
12. copper
13. Spain
14. knobs
15. decorations

INCAN ROADS AND BRIDGES–QUESTIONS (page 61)
1. 10,000
2. Royal Road
3. coastal highway
4. 24 feet
5. side walls to keep out sand drifts and mark roads
6. tampus
7. bridge
8. maguey
9. reeds
10. basket on a cable pulled across a river

INCAN ROADS AND BRIDGES–WORD SEARCH (page 62)

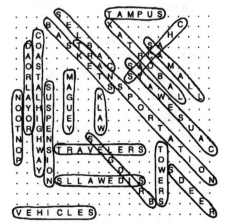

CITIES OF THE INCAS–QUESTIONS (page 64)

1. central plaza
2. large, stone fortresses
3. used no cement
4. trapezoid; wider at the bottom than the top
5. with solid gold
6. Cuzco
7. A.D. 1100
8. Machu Picchu
9. 1911
10. terraces

CITIES OF THE INCAS–CROSSWORD (page 65)

THE INCA AND HIS GOVERNMENT–QUESTIONS (page 67)

1. Inca
2. The people believed he was a descendant of the gods.
3. coya
4. by a council of the nobles
5. borla; fringe of bright cords ending in gold tubes
6. servants carried him on a litter of gold
7. palace; dead ruler buried in old one
8. mummies were worshiped
9. Cuzco
10. labor service or tax that government required of all Incan men

THE INCA AND HIS GOVERNMENT–WORD SCRAMBLE (page 68)

1. descendant
2. coya
3. council of nobles
4. borla
5. litter
6. canopy
7. palace
8. mummies
9. Cuzco
10. mita
11. Inti
12. crown
13. shrine
14. absolute power
15. empire

THE LLAMA: THE ANIMAL OF THE INCAS– QUESTIONS (page 70)

1. llama
2. camel
3. 300 pounds
4. adapts well to high altitudes
5. 100–130 pounds
6. faster than a horse
7. blankets, ropes, and sacks
8. sandals
9. dried llama meat
10. still used as they were by Incas, in Andes Mountains

THE LLAMA: THE ANIMAL OF THE INCAS–WORD SEARCH (page 71)

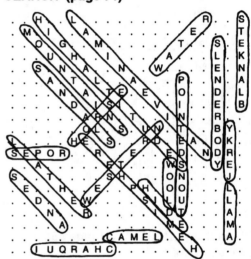

THE INCAS AND THE SPANISH CONQUEST– QUESTIONS (page 73)

1. had little contact with Mayas and Aztecs
2. ruler Huyayna Capac died without choosing an heir
3. five years
4. Atahualpa
5. A European captured on the Brazilian coast
6. May 13, 1532
7. Pizarro
8. horses
9. didn't want to offend them; thought they might be gods
10. prison cell

THE INCAS AND THE SPANISH CONQUEST–CROSSWORD (page 74)

THE AZTECS–QUESTIONS (page 77)

1. the territory called Aztlan
2. Valley of Mexico
3. Tenochtitlan
4. Mexico City
5. Nahuatl
6. picture writing
7. Montezuma or Moctezuma or Motecuhzoma
8. calpolli
9. searching for gold
10. Cortés

AZTEC DAILY LIFE–QUESTIONS (page 81)

1. sauna
2. Telpuchalli
3. boys and girls
4. loincloth and sometimes cloak
5. the maguey plant and cotton
6. answers vary: chocolate (most likely answer for like to eat)
7. answers vary: dog (most likely answer for not like to eat)

8. C	12. F
9. H	13. A
10. G	14. B
11. E	15. D

AZTEC DAILY LIFE–WORD SCRAMBLE (page 82)

1. adobe	11. Calmecac
2. patio	12. maguey
3. craftsman	13. jade
4. weaving	14. steam
5. loincloth	15. Telpuchalli
6. maize	
7. chili peppers	
8. tortilla	
9. chicle	
10. chocolate	

AZTEC SOCIETY–QUESTIONS (page 84)

1. the basis of all Aztec society
2. tribe
3. calpolli
4. council
5. civil and religious affairs
6. war matters
7. enforcing laws
8. book of fate, to see if the birth date was lucky or not
9. 13
10. the cloaks of the bride and groom

AZTEC SOCIETY–CROSSWORD (page 85)

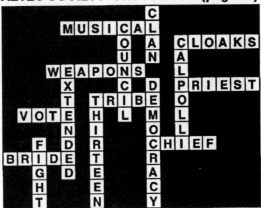

AZTEC RELIGION–QUESTIONS (page 88)

1. Ochpanizti
2. the Aztec mother earth goddess
3. patron god or goddess
4. a basket of corn
5. sacred chants
6. human sacrifices
7. young men dressed in their finest ceremonial outfits
8. Knights of the Eagle, Knights of the Jaguar
9. wore animal skins to represent their mascots
10. tlachti

AZTEC RELIGION–WORD SEARCH (page 89)

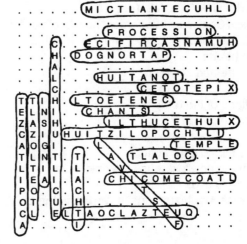

THE AZTEC CALENDAR–QUESTIONS (page 92)
1. Moon
2. 13
3. 20
4. by looking at the lunar calendar and deciding if the day was lucky or not
5. movement of the Sun
6. 365
7. 18
8. 20
9. They considered them unlucky, stopped all activities on those five days, and didn't name them
10. calendar stone

THE CITY OF TENOCHTITLAN–QUESTIONS (page 95)
1. on an island in Lake Texcoco
2. twin village, Tlaltelolco
3. canals
4. large earthen causeways
5. its own section of the city
6. the great plaza
7. over 200 feet tall
8. a dream
9. 200,000–300,000 people; none
10. Mexico City

THE CITY OF TENOCHTITLAN–CROSSWORD (page 96)

AZTEC ART–QUESTIONS (page 98)
1. of goddess Coatlicue; two serpent heads, claws for hands and feet, skirt of snakes, necklace of human hands and hearts
2. architecture and sculpture
3. temple
4. decorations of the temple
5. gods and animals
6. stone
7. calendar stone, over 20 tons
8. melted them down to reuse the gold
9. raised exotic birds
10. headdress Montezuma gave Cortés is the only one

AZTEC ART–WORD SCRAMBLE (page 99)
1. serpents
2. Coatlicue
3. Tenochtitlan
4. sculpture
5. turquoise
6. jade
7. jewelry
8. clay pottery
9. feather weaving
10. headdress
11. Montezuma
12. calendar
13. emerald
14. Cortés
15. spiders

AZTEC GAMES–QUESTIONS (page 101)
1. tlachtli
2. Mayan game of pok-a-tok
3. seven
4. like a snake
5. like a capital "I"
6. to put a ball through a ring
7. hard rubber
8. with their hands
9. patolli
10. beans with dots painted on them

AZTEC AGRICULTURE–QUESTIONS (page 104)
1. plow; planting stick
2. ashes from burnt trees and bushes
3. small hills or mounds made by scraping mud into piles and used for farming swamps and lowlands
4. floating gardens
5. maize or corn
6. cacao beans
7. on their backs
8. dugout canoes
9. Cortés
10. barter system

AZTEC AGRICULTURE–WORD SCRAMBLE (page 105)
1. cacao beans
2. cotton
3. tomatoes
4. maize
5. papayas
6. beans
7. squashes
8. sweet potatoes
9. rubber
10. avocados
11. chinampas
12. fertilizer
13. terraces
14. Tlatelolco
15. barter

AZTEC MEDICINE–QUESTIONS (page 107)

1. religion, belief in magical powers, and use of plants and herbs to make medicine
2. angry gods and goddesses, enemies' black magic, nature
3. to ward off harm and evil
4. doctor or shaman
5. to remove magic darts thought to cause illness
6. plants, roots, herbs, bark
7. yauhtli and iztauhyatl
8. sap from the maguey plant
9. volcanic glass
10. according to Cortés, as good as Spanish doctors

AZTEC MEDICINE–WORD SEARCH (page 108)

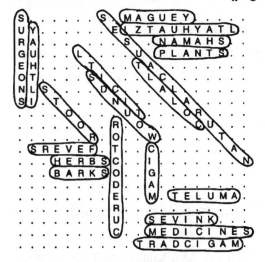

AZTEC WARFARE–QUESTIONS (page 110)

1. it was believed to be a religious duty
2. at a school called the telpuchalli
3. followed warriors into battle
4. social rank, land, or important offices
5. a sword edged with pieces of obsidian glass
6. yes; padded cotton
7. Warriors didn't use animals to carry extra supplies; when the food ran out, the battle was over.
8. the first to retreat lost
9. to get tribute and human sacrifices
10. capture the enemy, not kill him

AZTEC WARFARE–CROSSWORD (page 111)

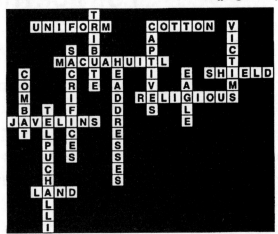

THE ARRIVAL OF THE SPANIARDS–QUESTIONS (page 113)

1. Cortés
2. Conquistadors
3. three years
4. Montezuma
5. 1521
6. Spanish had better weapons and armor
7. sent them to Spain
8. smallpox
9. Inca
10. 12 years; 176 years

THE ARRIVAL OF THE SPANIARDS–WORD SCRAMBLE (page 114)

1. new world
2. expedition
3. Conquistadors
4. Montezuma
5. treasures
6. missionaries
7. smallpox
8. Spaniards
9. infection
10. invaders
11. Quetzalcoatl
12. religion
13. prisoner
14. Incas
15. Mayas

FOR FURTHER READING

For older readers:

Berdan, Frances F. *The Aztecs*, (The Indians of North America Series). Chelsea House, 1989.

Bray, Warwick. *Everyday Life of the Aztecs*. Dorsett Press, 1987.

Brunhouse, Robert L. *In Search of the Maya*. Ballantine Books, 1990.

Cameron, Ian. *Kingdom of the Sun God: a History of the Andes and their People*. Facts on File, 1991.

Divan, T. *Aztecs and Mayas*. Gordon Press, 1976.

Everyday Life of the Incas, (Everyday Life Series). Dorset Press, 1990.

Gruzinski, Serge. *The Aztecs: Rise and Fall of an Empire*. Harry N. Abrams Inc., 1992.

Indians of the Andes; Incas, Aymaras and Quechuas. Gordon Press, 1977.

Morlaes, Demetrio S. *The Maya World*. Ocelot Press, 1976.

Sharer, Robert J. *The Ancient Maya*. Stanford University Press, 1994.

For younger readers:

Baquedano, Elizabeth. *The Aztec, Inca and Maya*, (Eyewitness Books). Knopf Books for Young Readers, 1993. (grades 5+)

Dineen, Jaqueline. *The Aztecs*, (Worlds of the Past Series). MacMillan Children's Book Group, 1992. (grades 6+)

Green, Jacqueline. *The Maya*, (First Books Series). Franklin Watts Inc., 1992. (Grades 5 to 8)

Kendall, Sarita. *The Incas*, (Worlds of the Past Series). MacMillan Children's Book Group, 1992. (grades 6+)

Newman, Shirley P. *The Incas*, (First Books Series). Franklin Watts Inc., 1992. (grades 5 to 8)

Odijk, Pamela. *The Mayas*, (Ancient World Series). Silver Burdett Press, 1990. (grades 5 to 8)

Shepherd, Donna W. *The Aztecs*, (First Books Series). Franklin Watts Inc., 1992. (Grades 5 to 8)

Wood, Tim. *The Aztecs*, (See Through History Series). Viking Children's Books, 1992. (grades 3 to 7)